SURVIVAL
A Widow's Journal

By Muriel Kagan Zager

Muriel Kagan Zager is also the author of

Bystander (1992)
*The Faithful (1997)
Death of a Pilgrim (2000)

Published by Strawberry Hill Press

Murder on the Mount of Olives (2006)

Published by Highlands Publications, Inc.

*Nominated for a National Book Award

For my daughters

Lynne Donna Zager
Susan Kagan Zager

CHAPTER 1

Hell Days

It all happened so quickly.

We returned to Tennessee on Sunday after visiting a new great-grand-child in Texas.

On Wednesday, Victor left for the airport at 4:00 a.m. to catch an early flight to Detroit and returned Thursday evening.

He seemed tired but didn't complain about feeling ill.

A miserable Memorial Day Weekend began that Saturday. Victor was in agony the entire time. Even though he had the physician's cell phone number, he wouldn't call the physician because he didn't want to disturb the doctor on a holiday.

Instead, he phoned the physician who was on call who offered something to relieve gas. It didn't help. My omeprazole pill helped a bit.

But Victor had trouble lying down so he slept sitting up in the chair in our bedroom. He told me that every time he looked over at me lying in our bed I was looking at him.

Of course I stayed awake watching him. I was worried.

Finally, Tuesday morning arrived and we went to the radiology building where he had a CT scan. The attendant told us to go to Victor's doctor's office. By then, Victor's stomach was so swollen he looked as if he were pregnant.

At the doctor's office we were given the news that there seemed little doubt that the spots they found were cancerous.

His doctor had him admitted to the hospital.
There, he was aspirated. I think they removed 3 liters of liquid.

<u>Tuesday to Friday in Bristol Regional Medical Center</u>

Watching him suffer was almost unbearable. Even though he was given morphine, he was in terrible pain. He was nauseous - throwing up. We used to joke about at a certain age one's parts fall apart. It came to mind because that's what seemed to be happening to him.

Victor didn't complain. Instead he repeated the phrase that, 'suffering never redeems but makes you worthy of redemption,' a quote he often used.
The swelling in his stomach grew worse and worse.
As I sat by his hospital bed, helpless, he moaned. He told me not to mind the moaning. Moaning made him feel better, he said.
My mind filled with many thoughts.
Laughing always helped us through the hard times. So we laughed.
But for me, facing him – me in a chair – him in that hospital bed, watching his face distorted in pain, I thought, there isn't enough laughter in the world to ease the agony I was feeling.
Somehow, watching him, I was reminded of the book: "As I Lay Dying." And I thought, as he lays dying the pain in the pit of my stomach tells me that in a way, I'm dying too.
If only that were true, that I too was dying it would make his dying easier for me, I thought.
He looked God-awful but kept working, talking on the phone, making notes, fooling around with the nurses and doctors, making jokes. The only time he broke down was when he heard that Richard, our grandson who was in Israel at the time, put a note in the Wall in Jerusalem asking for Victor's healing.
That broke him up.

CHAPTER 2

~⁓⁓

The Trip To Nashville

The family decided that we should Air Med Victor to Nashville where the facility might be better equipped to treat him.

Although we had insurance to cover it, his doctor would not file the correct form because the insurance form said the coverage only applied if death was imminent. His doctor thought that was not true in Victor's case.

The cost was outrageous.

Actually, I believed the reason his doctor wouldn't sign the form was because his doctor didn't want to give up his patient. The doctor claimed they could do just as good a job for Victor in the regional hospital in Bristol, although that facility had limited services.

Nevertheless, the family was determined to get him to Nashville and a state of the art facility at any cost. Family reasoning went this way: there was an 80th surprise birthday planned for Victor by the family. The invitations were already out.

"If need be we'll serve chicken instead of filet mignon at the party," our daughter Lynne declared.

Victor was busy on the phone trying to make arrangements to fly commercially, or have a car drive him from Bristol to Nashville, so as not to incur that cost. Despite his doctor insisting Victor could fly commercially or be driven to Nashville, we all felt that Victor could not survive the trip any other way but by a medically equipped plane.

David, our son, spoke with the Air Med insurance people who were adamant that death had to be imminent. So David asked, "Does imminent mean that you fly the patient directly to heaven?"

They didn't see the humor in that. We did.

Although it wasn't covered, our son and daughters arranged for the Air Med flight, anyway.

I went home to pack, opened the front door, disarmed the alarm and a primal scream crept up through my body and escaped my mouth. It was unexpected, loud and frightening. I couldn't believe it came out of me.

After that outburst, I calmly packed. A full suitcase for him, filled with all the clothes he requested; a few things for me.

A friend picked me up, and brought me back to the hospital. There, I was a calm and controlled human being ready for the trip to Nashville.

That trip proved to be quite an experience.

A Bristol ambulance crew arrived at the hospital with a medic, a nurse, the flight crew of three and a gurney.

They got Victor onto the gurney, attached a heart monitor to him and some intravenous drips. With two suitcases sitting on a ledge at the bottom of the gurney, the seven of us rolled the gurney, with Victor attached to all the equipment, into the hall, into the elevator and out of the hospital.

The crew asked me if I had ever flown before. I laughed. Victor and I had flown the world over and had plans for three upcoming trips abroad.

Later on, I wondered why the pilot would ask such a question. According to that crew, most people they took into the plane had never flown before.

I sat with Victor in the back of the ambulance, along with the nurse, the medic and a female from the ambulance service. They offered me a more comfortable seat in the front, but I wasn't about to leave Victor for a moment. I announced that despite the fact that I was a million-miler on airplanes I had never been in an ambulance before (although I had actually been in one with an injured neighbor's child years ago.) I thought my joke re: plane versus ambulance might get a laugh. It did.

Lightening situations such as that one with humor was the way I always coped. I felt that even if it did not help others just going through the attempt, helped me.

When we arrived at the airport, the gurney was placed directly into the plane. The co-pilot gave me instructions about how to buckle a safety belt, and all the other announcements one is given on a commercial flight. So I jokingly asked him if he was going to serve peanuts. He said no.

The pilot was a woman and she spoke to Victor, explaining the procedure and how we would be flying. He was pleased that the pilot was a woman and told her so.

They made Victor as comfortable as they could. All during the flight they gave him medication when he was in pain and monitored him all the way. But he was having a difficult time. Was it the altitude? I didn't know. But he was in pain, nauseous and extremely uncomfortable, proving he could never had withstood a five-hour car trip or a commercial flight to Nashville.

About one hour later, we arrived in Nashville. The gurney was removed from the plane and slid into a waiting ambulance. I was told to sit in the front with the driver. I would not be allowed in the back but there was a video screen on the dashboard so I could observe everything that was going on in the back.

When we arrived at St. Thomas Hospital, the gurney was rolled directly into building where staff was waiting. They placed a wristband with an ID on him and gave me a paper telling me how someone could call the room he would be in. I had been concerned that checking into the hospital would be complicated and time consuming. It took a total of several seconds.

There we were in Nashville where we had planned to be on that Friday evening for our grandson's High School graduation. When Victor was wheeled into his room, sitting by the window was our daughter Susan. She greeted us with, "You're just on time for the graduation."

Frankly, with all that had gone on for the past few days I had completely forgotten about the graduation. But once again, we were able to laugh.

CHAPTER 3

~⁊

St. Thomas Hospital

From the moment Victor was placed in his bed at the St. Thomas Hospital doctors of every specialty arrived.

The numerous professionals asked many questions. Blood tests were taken, IV was administered, and an EKG was given.

A woman physician, who was the daughter-in-law of our daughter Lynne's friend was the admitting physician and oversaw the entire course of action, wrote orders for several specialists to visit Victor and for tests to be made.

These procedures began at our arrival on Friday evening and continued during the entire weekend.

Doctors kept coming in to see Victor, which was good. Only the reports were not. One after the other declared, 'you have pneumonia; you're dehydrated; you're anorexic; your breathing is poor; your this is failing, your that is failing. Etc, etc.' Results of every test he took turned out negative.

One morning his physician asked him, "How are you today?"

With a smile on his lips he responded, "They're trying to depress me but I won't let them."

Throughout the weekend the family came to visit. Almost all of his grandchildren were able to see and speak with him during those days.

He greeted each in his turn. Victor was happy to see them and had beautiful times with all of them, making sure each one had an exclusive moment with his grandfather.

One grandchild in particular was plainly discomforted being in the room and watching Victor failing. The child didn't say anything and hung out in a corner where he did not need to look at the bed. Victor made the child talk to him. That grandchild left kissing his grandfather on the cheek and telling him he would see him soon.

Other grandchildren seemed to hold their own with Victor. Every grandchild was able to communicate with Victor and express his love of him. And Victor was able to do the same. Beauty and love flowed in that hospital room.

By Monday, he was taken for another test but was too weak and too ill to take it. When he returned to his room he asked the doctor if there were other tests that he could take.

She answered no. His body couldn't go through any more, she said. It was a matter of time.

What was so very hard for me to fathom was that several days' earlier life seemed normal.

A couple of weeks earlier we were dancing at a wedding; we had gone to Texas to meet a new great-grandchild; we had three oversees trips planned for the next few months.

How could all this be happening?

In my mind, which was a jumble trying to accept what was going on, different tunes and words kept circulating.

One was:
> "Those were the days my friend
> We thought they'd never end
> We'd sing and dance forever and a day
> We'd live the life we choose
> We'd fight and never lose
> Those were the days, oh yes those were the days."

Another was: "Is that all there is?
> "Is that all there is?"

If that's all there is my friend
Then let's keep dancing."

Allan, a close friend who flew in from Boston to be at Victor's bedside announced, "I'm not going to wait until you die to tell you what I think of you, Zager."

He then proceeded to tell Victor all the loving thoughts he had and the high esteem in which he held his friend whom he cherished like a brother.

It was wonderful that each of our children were able to spend some quality time with Victor.

David, our son, told his father, "Father, as in the book Ethics of the Fathers, you are a righteous man."

Victor never lost his sense of humor or his warm, pleasant personality.

At one point Victor thought that maybe he should take a walk. Then Susan suggested he first have some matzo ball soup she had bought. He had not been eating but he said he would try to do that.

When it seemed as if he was through eating the tiny amount he had in his bowl, I asked him what he wanted to do now, wondering if he still wanted to take a walk.

His answer was, "I want to finish my matzo ball soup."

We all laughed.

Then there was the blue pen hunt. Victor wanted to make some changes in his will. All the papers were prepared and a friend, who was a notary, was at Victor's hospital bed as were two nurses who would act as witnesses.

But Victor wouldn't sign the papers because he insisted that his signature had to be in blue ink. As a lawyer he felt strongly that this was the way to ensure that the papers were original and legal. They could not be copied because the signature would appear in black ink.

Each of the family members went scurrying through the hospital in search of a blue pen. We checked with staff as well as visitors and a blue pen could not be found. Finally, when we were about to give up a visitor in the waiting room exclaimed that she had a blue pen. Seemingly it was the only blue pen in the building. We rushed the pen to Victor's bedside and he finally signed the papers. He smiled. We breathed a sigh of relief.

Since then, I believe everyone in our family carries a blue pen with them wherever they go.

David, Susan and I had a particularly poignant moment with Victor who asked us to join hands. When we did, he gave us the priestly blessing.

The priestly blessing is a Hebrew blessing also known in Hebrew as Nesiat Kapayim or Raising of the Hands. It is a Jewish prayer coming from God himself recited during certain Jewish services. It is based on a scriptural verse: "They shall place My name upon the children of Israel, and I Myself shall bless them."

It consists of the following Biblical verses from Numbers 6:24-26:

May God bless you and guard you

May God make his face shine upon you and be gracious unto you

May God lift up his face onto you and give you peace

Unfortunately Lynne missed that moment. She was at the airport picking up Richard, her son, who had flown in from Israel where he had spent one half of a high school term studying. He returned to America early in order to see his grandfather.

By Tuesday, we were trying to get Victor a room in hospice that was located inside the hospital. The doctors convinced us it was what we needed to do.

David and I checked it out, and we were going to make the arrangements when the doctors now told us that we didn't have time to move him.

Victor asked David, his wife Kitzi and I to go to the cemetery to pick out the spot we wanted for the family plot we had purchased. He wanted us to pick out a spot like the kind he had in mind. He wanted our plots to be located near a tree. I knew why.

I remembered the time when Victor and I went with Victor's father to pick out the location for the family plot in New York. Victor's father wanted those plots to be near a tree. Victor had the same request in mind; he wanted our plots in Tennessee to be located near a tree. But He also wanted Kitzi to go with us because, he reasoned, she would be buried there along side her husband and she should have a say in the matter. We found a family plot near a tree.

When we returned to the hospital one of his physicians told us that it was a matter of hours.

We needed a miracle. It never came.

CHAPTER 4

My Moments With Victor

During the last five days of his life, I had my alone time with Victor.

I told him that this was a real kick in the head.

He said when he first heard the news he thought we would have a six month transition period.

I asked him if this was difficult. He said no it isn't difficult.

I remember thinking what an extraordinary life we'd had and wondering who could ask for any more? ME! I answered myself.

He said, hold my hand while I sleep.

We had traveled the world together holding hands.

My tears overflowed as I sat holding his hand and watched his life fading. How will I survive without him, I wondered?

I wish I could go with you, I said. I said you never take me anywhere. Of course that wasn't true.

I take you everywhere that's important, he said. Which was more than true.

Hold my hand, he'd say, again. And then he'd kiss my hand.

I said I love you and he said I love you more ways than I can count.

When I saw his blood pressure drop to 76/38 I suspected we only had a few more days.

I was reminded what Victor always advised, "Stay out of hospitals and courtrooms. They dissipate your energy and you rarely get what you want."

As he was dying, vignettes of our life popped into my mind.

While watching him one hour, I suddenly remembered that this was the day we were to leave for Amsterdam and then go on to Paris.

Amsterdam. Just thinking of that city brought back memories. I could see us walking; I could see the canals; see the shops; see the people eating outdoors; watch folks in the cafes; remembered one café on the rooftop of a building. It all looked beautiful and alive.

Through most of our walks through life whether on beaches or in cities, we always held hands.

Often, in the hospital we held hands.

One time, when he squeezed mine, I thought of sitting in the theater in London watching the show "Carousel." He took my hand when the song "If I Loved You" began. He squeezed my hand that time too.

Suddenly I realized that we had been at that theater just a few months earlier.

Waves of sadness would engulf me as I relived those beautiful memories of a beautiful love.

It felt like no one else in the world had a love like mine or a lover like mine.

Although the memories warmed me, I felt that the blood had been drained out of me, and I was flooded with a lifetime of memories.

So, as he lay dying I thanked him for a wonderful life.

I told him how much I loved him

He squeezed my hand- I squeezed his.

One of those times Victor asked me to stay with him.

"Don't leave me," he said. I told him I'd never leave him and begged him not to leave me.

His answer was, "We'll always have Paris."

One evening, while I was trying to decide whether to go back to our son's house with the family or stay in the hospital with him. He advised me to do what's best for the family. He always put the family first.

I never understood what he saw in me. He had so much more to offer than I did.

Before we married he cleaned out his savings account in order to buy me diamonds. At that time he told me that he bought the engagement ring and diamond wedding band because he didn't know if he would ever be able to afford to buy them again.
But he bought many more after that.

Financially, we started our life together with less than nothing. We were really two children. Working since the age of twelve, Victor, with hard work, built a successful and rich life.

And he was always kind to widows, making a special effort to look after them, to include them.

I realized that my life was over – abruptly- but it was over. In order to move on I had to create a new life, find out who this new me was, and where I fit into the universe.
There was no way to go back to the old life. So I kept telling myself: 'Can't go around it, can't go over it, have to go through it.'
But doing it was very difficult.

Every once in a while he would look at me, smile and repeat the words, "hazak, hazak," with that, the Hebrew word for strength, he was offering me courage.

He made me strong. With him I felt strong.

Fifty-six years.

I said it was a hell of a ride, Zager. He responded yeah, "Two kids from Brooklyn."

Susan and I slept in his room the night before he died. I was on the floor; she was in the chair. Sleeping is not what we really did. Knowing the end was near we spent the night watching him. I kissed him on the lips around 12:00 midnight that last night.

In the morning, we continued to watch him.

I asked Susan to let me sit in the chair for a while. She sat in a folding chair opposite me. For one brief moment, neither of us was looking at him. When I did, I said to my daughter, "He's gone."

He had taken that moment to spare us seeing him go.

I rang for the nurse; Susan ran for a nurse.

I kissed him on the lips in the morning around 7:00 a.m. moments after he died.

He looked so peaceful in death.

Victor died with grace, dignity, courage and strength.

Although I didn't know how or even if I could, I decided I had to try to live my life that way.

CHAPTER 5

Making Funeral Arrangements

Susan came into the room with a nurse a few minutes later. The nurse said that I could stay in the room with Victor as long as I wanted. I spent a few moments alone with my husband; Susan made some calls.

David and Kitzi joined Susan and me at the hospital and we linked up with Lynne and Toby at a Starbucks nearby. We discussed certain aspects of the funeral and David reached the rabbi who was on a trip but would be back in time to perform the service on Friday. The rabbi wanted us to meet him at the synagogue before the funeral to go over some things. He asked us to each make notes about Victor, whom he didn't know.

When we left the coffee shop and were walking to the car, I turned to Susan and without thinking said, "Wait. Where's your father? We have to wait for your father." It seemed so normal. When I realized what I had said, I felt I must be losing my mind.

At the funeral home we worked as a family making decisions we thought Victor would be pleased with. I viewed the casket to make sure it was a plain wooden one; we wrote the obit for the newspapers; we bought memorial candles for each of us; and as is our tradition, I arranged to have someone wash, stay with his body, and read psalms until Victor would be buried.

Although I had always been fortunate to have the capacity to relive events I had gone through in a way that is similar to viewing a TV screen or a movie, I cannot remember what we did the rest of the day. I vaguely remember calls being made and received. I even remember talking to people as far away as Israel. I remember emails being sent and received, food served. But it is all a blur.

I know this was the email sent to friends and relatives because I have a copy of it.

Dear friends,
Early this morning, Victor Zager lost his battle with pancreatic cancer and passed away peacefully, surrounded by his family. His illness moved very quickly and we are all grieving such a sudden loss.

A memorial service will be held at 2:00 p.m. on Friday, June 6, 2008 at Congregation Micah, on Old Hickory Boulevard in Nashville, Tennessee. Funeral arrangements are being handled by Marshall, Donnelly, and Combs Funeral Home. If you have questions regarding the service, they will be happy to take your call at (615) 327-1111.

In lieu of flowers, please make donations in honor of Victor Zager to:
Akiva Community Day School
809 Percy Warner Boulevard
Nashville, TN 37205
Tel: (615) 356-1880

We appreciate your support during such a difficult time.
Love,
The Zager Family

Everything was now set for what I was (in my mind) calling, "The Event." The funeral.

CHAPTER 6

Disassociation

A strange thing happened to me on the way to the funeral. I lost a day and a half. And I didn't even realize it until several months later.

All the time we spent in the funeral parlor is perfectly clear. I can visualize the family gathered around the table making all the arrangements.

I remember discussing the obituary, what it should say and where it should appear. I remember talking on the phone to a man at the synagogue who would arrange to have someone ritually cleanse Victor's body and to sit with the body around the clock saying psalms and prayers until the funeral on Friday morning. I can recall all of those details, down to my viewing the casket.

After that, nothing. I lost a day and a half.

The rest of Wednesday is lost. And Thursday doesn't exist at all in my memory. It's as if I went directly from the funeral home to the synagogue and the meeting with the Rabbi on Friday just prior to the funeral.

Many months later, a good friend, Bonnie, visited with me and filled me in on the details.

It seems Bonnie and her husband arrived on Wednesday, hoping to see Victor. But it was too late. Bonnie remembered seeing me in the car and remembered visiting at David's house where I was staying with the family and others who had joined us after we returned from the funeral parlor.

She told me things I spoke about, like a plant arriving from someone in Bristol. We thought that was odd because the person sending it wasn't a friend; she told me how I joked about Susan, of all people turning into a Jewish mother at the hospital, taking care of Victor and all of us; how I spoke about Victor dying; how she and I laughed and cried and how other friends arrived on Wednesday, Thursday and Friday.

In my mind everyone arrived on Friday morning for the funeral.

The facts Bonnie gave me sounded vaguely familiar, but I was not there. I can recall none of it. Me, the person who can vividly not only recall but can watch past events unfold before my eyes many days, weeks, months, or years later. Those events play in my mind as if I am watching a rerun of a TV series. Yet somehow, that period of time is not there for me.

The mind is amazing. And at times like those, I suppose the pain was too severe and so my mind protected itself. I simply mentally left the situation.

Another friend, Barbara, who is a therapist, and has helped me through this journey, explained that I disassociated.

Barbara had brought that up with me shortly after I arrived back in Bristol after the funeral. I explained that I wasn't hearing some things, wasn't seeing some things. After I told her exactly what I went through with those episodes she labeled it not a hearing or loss of sight loss, but a disassociation.

What I hadn't realized until a year later was that I had also disassociated away an entire day and a half.

CHAPTER 7

~⌐

The Event

About the funeral, I have total recall of the day. I remember clearly every detail. It was and is as if the day is unfolding before my eyes.

As I mentioned earlier, the rabbi had requested the family gather at the synagogue for a meeting with him and we were there. David, Lynne, Susan, Toby and I gathered.

Also, at the rabbi's request, we each wrote notes about Victor and brought them with us.

Here are the notes I carried with me:

From the psalms; the Song of Solomon: I was my beloved; my beloved was me.

I am my beloved, and my beloved is mine.

Victor earned a degree in theology and was well versed in Christianity as well as Judaism,

He was friends with Christians, Hindus, Palestinians, Armenians, etc.

We traveled to Israel twice a year.

Victor was responsible for the acquisition of the Synagogue in Jerusalem. It was originally a church.

He set up an endowment for Holocaust studies at Emery and Henry College in memory of his father.

And a lectureship at ETSU for a series on religious diversity was established by him.

Victor was ethical in business. He always maintained that he wanted to leave, to conclude every transaction, making sure all the parties were happy.

He often said: "I've seen the future and it doesn't work. You have to have good people to make it work".

He loved to talk to all people. He loved to talk to waiters, chambermaids anyone in his path in Spanish, Arabic, Italian, French, and to watch as their faces lit up.

We were walking in the Nashville Airport one time and he saw an Arab who was cleaning the floor. He stopped and said, "Sabachear" an Arab greeting. They had a conversation. The man was overcome with joy.

The Tennessee regional president of the DAR called last night to say how much she loved him.

He was blessed with a great sense of humor.

And he was equally at home with Rabbis, Ministers, Priests, Imams, Doctors, clerks, Chambermaids.....

Of course many of the things I jotted down, the family had on their lists as well. But it gave us an opportunity to talk about him and to each add our voice to help the rabbi know a little bit about this extraordinary man.

It also gave us an opportunity to remember.

We left the rabbi, went back to David's home and prepared to go to the Temple where the funeral took place.

At David's home I walked in and all the children and grandchildren were there as were Parker and Zachery our great grandsons. They were all dressed so beautifully and looked so wonderful, I could hardly bear it. It was their way of honoring Victor.

CHAPTER 8

Celebration Of His Life

A few days after the funeral, I returned home - alone. Despite my family's concern I insisted that I had to face this new journey by myself. Besides, remembering my primal scream when I returned to the house to pack, I was concerned about how I would react walking into the house without him. I didn't want anyone, least of all the family, to see me that way.

But before that hurdle, I had to face flying home alone. Feeling empty and completely vulnerable, somehow I got through it. Not easily, but I made it.

When I walked out of the plane and stepped into the lobby of the airport, waiting for me was Rod, the owner of the limousine service we used almost from the day he started the company. He hugged me and tears flowed down his face.

"I promised myself I would not break up," he said. But he did. And he was one of the first of many I ended up consoling for their loss.

It was easier to come through the door of my home than I expected it to be. I didn't scream, as I feared I might. Perhaps I was simply numb.

"This is it," I told myself. "This is definitely the beginning of this new journey." At that point I wished it had been the end of my journey. Frankly, I didn't want to go on.

Two days later I decided that I needed to allow our friends in Bristol, who were unable to make the journey to Nashville, to pay their respects, to have the opportunity to do so.

I held what I called, A Celebration of His Life, and thought of it as: the Second Event. I contacted a few people and told them to spread the word that I would be home at 2:00 on Saturday for those who wished to come.

Friends arranged for catering by a local restaurant and at 2:00 o'clock the people arrived.

I prepared a few words to explain what happened. Most of those gathered were in shock because the last time they saw him, some as little as two weeks earlier, Victor seemed in such good health. I gave a summation of the last few days of Victor's life.

This is what I prepared and read:

I want you all to know that I insisted my family not be here because I wanted this time alone with you.

My family arrives tomorrow.

I thought we should all get together to celebrate Victor's life. But first there are a few things you should know about his death, from my perspective.

He came home from a business trip to Detroit on May 22 just before Memorial Day Weekend.

A CT scan was administered on Friday and spots showed up in several areas.

He had fluid on his stomach and some was removed for testing. It was thought if we could determine where the cancer was located it could possibly be treated.

Victor spent the weekend in horrible pain. On Tuesday, he saw his doctor who thought he should be hospitalized. He was admitted to Bristol Regional and was aspirated. They removed three liters of fluid.

He spent the next two days having tests but although he was being made comfortable we had no test results. We decided to take him to Nashville to a hospital that has better resources and to a city where our family lives.

We flew him by plane on an Airmed flight. He admitted afterwards he could never have made the trip any other way.

During the next few days he was seen by gastroenterologists, oncologists, kidney specialists, etc, etc. By then he had pneumonia, too.

Things went from bad to worse as each part of his body was shutting down. He could no longer tolerate even simple tests.

One morning his oncologist asked how he was feeling and he said, "They're trying to depress me and I won't let them."

On Tuesday, June 3, he was told that he should consider going to hospice because it was a matter of days. Our son and I checked out the facility attached to the hospital and gave Victor our assessment. We all agreed, that it would probably be best.

Arrangements were being made for hospice when we were informed that things were moving more quickly. By then it was a matter of hours. Plans for hospice were canceled.

He was surrounded during his stay with his children, a close friend from Boston who considered Victor a brother, grandchildren and their spouses; one grandchild flew in from Israel, another grandchild from Texas with our great grandchild, still another drove from Atlanta.

He never lost his sense of humor or his will to live. Each member of the family had some very special moments with Victor before he died.

I told him we had quite a ride and he responded, "Yeah. Two kids from Brooklyn." He and I shared some very precious moments together. At one point he said, "We'll always have Paris."

He even evoked the priestly blessing to our children and me.

One of our daughters, Susan, and I spent the night at his bedside. He was comfortable He fought like the dickens but finally lost the fight the following morning, June 4 at 7:00 a.m. He died with dignity, courage, strength and grace.

His funeral was a traditional Jewish event. His grandchildren, all eleven of them, acted as pallbearers.

Our son, David, our daughter, Susan, Lynne's daughter, Rachel, age 13, and Allan gave eulogizes.

The first thing I told the rabbi about Victor was from the Song of Solomon:

I am my beloved's, and my beloved is mine:

Victor left us all with the Hebrew words: Hazak, Hazak, which means strength, strength.

That's what I'm trying to do now in his honor. I am trying to be strong. I have to start a whole new life and I despise the fact that I have to do so. But with your help, I will be able to succeed.

We've had wonderful phone calls and beautiful letters and emails from around the world. If you would like to say a few words, or share a story about Victor and his relationship with you, now's the time.

And sharing they did. The love and tears poured out.

A young doctor friend and client recalled that a couple of weeks earlier Victor was running up the stairs to his office and our friend couldn't keep up with him.

People of all ages from teens to 80's poured out their hearts.

Another friend read an email that he had earlier sent me.

A FRIEND'S TRIBUTE TO VICTOR ZAGER

Victor was my mentor.

He was always the final word on my questions about Judaism, but I will always think of Victor Zager and Muriel Kagan Zager together and I cannot separate their influences on me. I write this tribute to Victor but she is a part of all I feel and write, and I honor her too at this grievous time...

First, Victor loaned me his special signed copy of Elie Wiesel's "Night" and then it was he who introduced me to Viktor Frankl and "Man's Search for Meaning". That book has been especially important to me in my own thinking about the meaning of life, and it has helped me understand and deal appropriately with some patient problems I encountered in my surgical practice.

Victor and Muriel gave me the most valuable resource of all, the "Pentateuch and Haftorahs" which I have studied for many productive hours and used in teaching at my own church,

They acquainted me with the calendar, gave me a beautiful edition one year, and shared with me their feelings about the special days and the High Holy Days.

They generously, freely, and willingly shared themselves with someone outside their faith and Victor always welcomed questions – the more difficult, the better. He also from time to time sent me clippings of rabbinical writings he thought would interest me, especially Rabbi Heschel.

We have attended for many years an elegant New Year's Day celebration in their lovely and hospitable home.

My prayers have been with you from the onset of this illness and my heart remains with you in your suffering at this tragic loss. I wish for Muriel and for all the Zagers all that is good and bright and happy and healthy for the future.

This friend was not the only one who referred to Victor as a mentor. It seems Victor was mentor to most of the people who were there. Tears flowed easily around the room as one by one events were recalled; deeds were recalled; Victor was recalled.

The last person to speak asked if he might recite the Lord's Prayer. I said yes, and he did so.

Effectively that was the way we ended the event. It had been a good tribute and a good venting for all who came.

We had refreshments and some stayed to clean up and store away any left-over food.

Eventually, they all left and I was alone.

CHAPTER 9

Changing My Routine

My family arrived the following day.

Immediately, they began doing what I needed them to do. At my request, they removed Victor's clothes from closets and drawers, filled large trash bags with them and brought them to the local charity.

I remembered visiting a friend years before Victor died, whose mother had died a few years previous to my visit. There I found his mother's hair on her brush, her clothes still in her closet, her room exactly the way she left it. I was determined not to make a shrine of Victor's belongings.

However, I did keep Victor's old, beat up, red Toyota. A car I would not ride in when he was alive because it was in such poor condition. The seat belts didn't work, the radio didn't work; as a matter of fact it was a marvel that the engine still ran. He loved it.

Somehow I felt comforted seeing that car in the driveway, parked where he left it. Without meaning to, or realizing it, I seemed to have made a shrine of his car.

Our son, who was also a lawyer, busied himself with dismantling Victor's office. It was a monumental job made easier, because Victor kept such excellent records, and was so well organized. Still, there was a mountain of work to do.

Victor was a collector. In our travels we collected many things. We displayed those objects throughout our home and in shelves going from our kitchen to our bedroom. And many places in between.

I would pass those items at least twice a day. My eyes would focus on a particular piece and I would remember where we were when we acquired it. Sometimes, a tear would fall, sometimes a smile would come to my face, but all in all they brought back lovely memories of happier times.

In my dressing room, I always had a display of photographs sitting atop my built in drawers. Those pictures were mostly of Victor and me taken in many places throughout our travels. Also, there were photos of Victor and me with members of the family. Those photos also were passed, several times during the day, with a mingling of joy and pain.

I found it interesting to discover that I would sometimes be unable to hear anything that was said to me. I had suffered a slight loss of hearing prior to Victor's death so I chalked it up to that. But what was really happening was that I was in a state where I didn't hear what I didn't want to hear, and didn't see what I didn't want to see. It was almost as if I could transport myself out from where I was physically and could build a wall around me. It was eerie. Still, it enabled me to block out what I deemed overwhelmingly painful. It was my mind protecting me. Disassociation was helping.

Around this time, I had lost my appetite for food, sex, sleeping and exercising; each of which had been an important and enjoyable part of my life. But I knew that I always functioned best when I had a daily routine. I knew I needed the discipline and the regime.

In my old life I would go the YMCA at 6:00 a.m., work out for an hour and a half, come home, have a bite of breakfast and then go into my office and work until lunch. I definitely had to change my routine.

I no longer wanted to be this smiling, happy, congenial person I always had been at the YMCA. I thought people would expect me to make jokes about myself, listen to their problems and generally be this pleasant agreeable human being I had been in my previous life. But I didn't feel pleasant or agreeable. I wanted to avoid the whole scene.

When I finally did return to the YMCA, it was at a different day and time and I stayed for a much shorter period thus avoiding people I had known for years. I knew I needed to be with people and to socialize, but I sought out friends I could be comfortable with and with whom I did not have to pretend that I hadn't changed.

I had changed. I was a different person.

CHAPTER 10

Bits And Pieces Of Emotions

As my purpose in writing this journal is to try to help others who are going through this pain, I thought the best way of describing my journey is to share some of the notes I kept. The notes explained my feelings and what was happening to me, around me, and in my mind.

One week after the burial I wrote.

I'm beginning a new life.
I must start a new life.
I hate starting a new life, but I must.
The rabbi says I shouldn't say I'm starting a new life. He says I am continuing my life in a different way.
I say it's like Victor would say: turn the page.
The rabbi says it's continuing the page.
He doesn't understand.
I have to start a new life because the old one is over.

Two weeks after the burial.

I received an email from a friend while I was in Nashville right after Victor died. She wrote: right now you're walking with God. When you come home I'll join you.

Making my bed perfectly in the morning has become a compulsion. Every corner has to be tucked in, just so. I also make myself get out of bed, get dressed and try to start the day. Otherwise, I suspect, I will never get out of bed or out of the house.

I've been catching up (or trying to) with some of the paper work. The overwhelming piles of mail just seem to grow. Also, I'm trying to put some of my notes re: this horrible period, into some kind of perspective.

Although the truth is that I'm not doing too much of that because I'm not ready to get into it yet.

Just bits and pieces of emotions on bits and pieces of paper.

The weekends are long (especially since I have been waking at 3:00 am and tossing until 6:00). I refuse to get out of bed before 6:00 because otherwise the day is impossibly long.

It will do me good to get out of the house. Thinking of going to the movies tomorrow. If I do, it will be to see "Indiana Jones." That would probably be the only level I could tolerate right now. This is all part of trying to set my new life in motion.

I am doing very well, considering the circumstances. But as Victor left me with the admonition: hazak, hazak, strong is what I am trying to be. Don't think it's easy, it's anything but easy. Still, as I have no alternative, I am trying to be strong and trying to move forward.

I've always had this ability to recreate in my mind's eye places and events. They enfold like I am going through past experiences now as if they were occurring in the present. It's like watching a movie or TV screen. Except I am in it. Only now the visions seem to come in spurts, when I least expect it.

I'm sitting and doing some work, when suddenly I am transported to London and Victor and I are crossing a street in a hurry to catch a play. It is raining but not hard and cars have their lights on. And just as unexpectedly as the vision appears, it is gone. But the pain in my stomach I've had since

Victor died becomes more severe, because I know I can never have those kinds of moments again.

Or, in my mind, I suddenly pass an antique store in Paris that leads to other antique stores in Paris. Remembering while he was dying he said, "We'll always have Paris." And so I do, in my memories. But the picture is blurry as the tears are uncontrolled.

Walking the world with Victor. Hand in hand.
A lifetime of memories.

CHAPTER 11

One Month And Beyond

Again a vision came to me. This time I was waiting outside a hotel. Not even sure I knew where. But it seemed as if it was a grand hotel in the United States.

At that moment another vision just popped in – the first one popped out.

Who am I?

I started out in life as Alfred Kagan's daughter. Then I was Victor Zager's wife. I had a few years as David, Lynne and Susan's mother. Now I am Victor Zager's widow. I don't like the word widow.

In all those 56 years I never figured out why he chose me, married me, loved me.

The days are incredibly long. The weekends are longer.

Another memory: Watching Victor and I walking from the San Diego Ferry after landing in Coronado. Walking because we thought the bus wasn't coming. Met a whole group of people from all over the country on that walk.

Eventually the bus did come and we all hopped on. Including some children. That was a fun time.

Why does my stomach drop and the pain increase when I think of some memory of a street in Amsterdam; we are walking and holding hands? Is it because I can never have those moments again?

I often said to an empty house, "Victor, You don't know how lonesome this is. I've spent my entire life with you."

Moaning makes me feel better. Funny, Victor said that when he was in the hospital, dying. I am saying that moaning makes me feel better as I am living.

Going on is harder than I thought it would be. There isn't enough wine or tears in this world to ease the agony.

I miss him so very much. It's so terribly lonely. And it's not just the loneliness, it's the aloneness. I have never lived alone before. When I married Victor I was living at my parents home.

At this point what else am I mourning except my loss? I do feel sorry for myself. I turn around to nobody and ask, "How could this happen to me?"

The flood of memories never ends.

No one shares our memories. Covering the Lebanese War. Lebanon: Sabra and Shatilla; at the border in, Marjaoun; discovering the windows had been blown out in the hotel in Metulla, Watching, through those empty windows, as ambulances constantly streamed by; staying up all night.

Music and words engulf me: "You were meant for me. I was meant for you. Nature patterned us and when she was done. You were all the good things rolled into one. You're like a plaintive melody. That never lets me be. I'm content the angels must have sent you and they meant you just for me."

The things I'll never do again and the places I'll never see again except in my memories and in my mind.

How do I live the rest of my life without him when I've lived my whole life with him?

We walked the world holding hands.

Seeing us crossing the street in London. Holding hands in front of the theater, heading toward Leicester Square.

July 2,2008 - This was an especially lousy day. So depressed that I had to flee the house. Went to SAM's and did a bit of shopping. Didn't realize till the next day that this was the end of Shloshim (30 days) Jewish period of mourning.

It's only been about a month. It feels like 20 years that I've been alone, without him.

It's interesting to learn that when you're alone there are no rules. You make the rules. That means there is good and bad in everything as I have always maintained.

Does it get worse before it gets better? (It feels that way). Or does it just never get better?

Oh the pain. Sometimes I think the mental anguish right now is worse than the physical pain I have in the pit of my stomach.

We had a wonderful, full and great life. I am still hearing from people (some I don't even know) who were touched either by our life together or something that Victor did for them. He helped so many, even changed some of their lives. It is all very gratifying.

The memories are both a comfort and a source of pain. The pain comes from knowing I will never be able to do those things again or share those experiences I had with anyone else. No one truly shares your memories except the person you're with when you make those memories.

Just happened to remember when we lived in Briarwood (50 plus years ago) Victor couldn't understand that I could play the piano but couldn't type. We laughed then. The thought of that moment made me laugh.

I made it through another night. Sometimes I don't think I will.

Decided that I'm not doing anything I don't feel like doing. Whether it's making a phone call or putting gas in the car or going out or coming in.

Now I make all the decisions myself. There is no one I'm account-able to any more. Never had that before. I am responsible for all my own actions. Solely, responsible. Very interesting. Very frightening.

Here it is just about seven weeks since he died and I am still comfort-ing others. Most seem to break down when they see me, or call me. He touched so many people in so many ways.

One morning I had a call from the sister of an Israeli friend, who is in her 90's. The sister was very comforting. She's been here. She knows and understands where I am. What I am going through.

Finally, I got the courage to call my Israeli friend. She told me that when she thinks of me she cries. I do the same when I think of her. We both realize we shall probably never see each other again.

On another afternoon a younger Israeli friend called and said she didn't know if she could handle the thought of not seeing Victor again. She loved him so much. When she heard my telephone message, she couldn't call me back because she couldn't talk.

Time is not healing as I was led to believe it would. Seems to me as time passes, slowly and painfully, it is more difficult.

He's in every corner of my mind and heart. Almost anything can trigger a memory of walking somewhere or eating or sitting somewhere. Each memory is more painful than the last because I realize I will never do those things again, or see those places again or be with him again.

Painful doesn't quite explain it. My life is shattered, broken, over.

Sometimes I yearn to just feel the warmth of his body next to mine. That's when the pain in the pit of my stomach is even worse than usual.

Melancholy, what does that mean? I think I feel melancholy all the time. Definition is: thoughtful or gentle sadness. But it's more than gentle. It's steep, deep, and bottomless. And that pain in the stomach never eases.

Also there's a feeling of nervousness. (Definition: dread or apprehension.) Yes, That's what it is. Apprehension. A sense of unease. Off-balance.
I could be in this new state forever.
Forever is a long time.

CHAPTER 12

~⌒

Eight Weeks Since The Day He Died

I attended my first funeral after Victor died. It was a difficult thing for me to do. But it was the funeral of someone I knew years ago. I felt I owed it to our past to attend.

Seeing the people who had not sent a card, or made a call or somehow expressed their condolences for my loss was especially hard. Suddenly, these people, these phonies, were falling all over themselves articulating their grave feelings about my loss.

One even had the audacity to say she hadn't had the chance to come and see me but was planning to call and make a visit soon. I never heard from her.

If there was one thing I could never tolerate it was a phony. I was truly disgusted by some of the obvious spurious fakes.

Of course there were people who were sincere at that funeral as well. Tho,se were people who had come to the Celebration of Victor's Life. They expressed concern. But they meant it. They gave me the courage to withstand being on a cemetery and going through a funeral.

And lo and behold a widow we had taken to dinner once a month for years after her husband died attended that funeral. Victor took care of her legal affairs during those years and never charged her a fee. I had heard nothing from her.

I suppose she didn't expect to see me at this funeral. She looked shocked, surprised to see me. She offered not one word to me. Even the woman who had just buried her husband had the good grace to say she had a card for me sitting on her table but didn't have the chance to send it. True or not, she at least acknowledged my loss.

Different people reacted in different ways to my widowhood and I found it interesting,albeit emotional at times, to take stock of those reactions and those people.

CHAPTER 13

~~

Random Days,
Random Thoughts

It occurred to me once agian that I spent my entire life belonging to some-one else. I was so and so's daughter; so and so's sister; so and so's wife; so and so's mother; so and so's grandmother; so and so's great-grandmother and now so and so's widow.

There's that terrible, dreaded word, again. Widow.

One morning while having another crying bout, I thought, this time this crying spell, while awful, was not as bad as it had been. Neverthe-less, it had come, as they all did, like a wave washing over me. That particular crying spell happened when I was changing the linens on our bed. Victor used to help with that. Many times he made the bed when I was working out. That's probably what triggered it, I thought. Still, why those triggers occurred and why I seemed to react so emotionally, I had no idea.

Trying to sort out my new life I once again realized that I had to keep busy. That meant creating a new routine, particularly for the weekends, which were undoubtedly the pits.

So I changed my schedule. As I was awakening at two and three o'clock in the morning, it seemed a good idea to get up, make coffee, and return to bed with a good book, read until six and then get dressed and go to the YMCA for my workout.

Following that I arranged to meet friends for lunch at a nearby restaurant. That helped to get through the day. It also gave me reasons to leave the house. I feared if I didn't, I might seclude myself in my home and never want to face the world.

Two months into my new life, I finally had a full night's sleep. But no sooner had I noted that realization, I was back to not sleeping very much the next night.

A friend suggested that I need an aim, a purpose to my life. I told her I already had one – to survive.

One particular morning Jefferson Keeler speaking on NPR's Writers Almanac remarked that Mary Roberts Rheinhart (the author whose book the N.Y. publisher reissued instead of publishing my first novel) said: "A little work, a little sleep, a little love and it's all over." I thought it very apropos of my situation.

My birthday was coming up and I had a pre-birthday song roaming around in my head:

All by myself I get lonely.
All by myself I get sad.
I want to rest my weary head on somebody's (read Victor) shoulder.
I hate growing older.
All by myself.

Difficult does not begin to describe the life I was living. How can anyone imagine how HARD this new existence was. In many ways it was getting harder the longer I was in it. Just when I would think it's going to get better, it didn't. As a matter of fact, it felt like it was getting more severe.

This new life trip I was on was not difficult; it was impossible. So I created a new motto: Can't go around it...can't go over it...have to go through it!!!

At the airport in Bristol the day I left for a friend's house in Falmouth, I saw a burley airport policeman Victor and I had befriended. I thought he was going to faint when I told him the news. He had to sit down. He was crying. This big, strong policeman, gun in holster, muscles on his arms, crying. He was so extremely emotional it shook me. But once again I was doing the consoling.

For me the entire trip was tough. I found myself crying non-stop.
I saw Victor everywhere. Kept wishing he was with me. I decided this life, this journey I was on was a journey from hell.

And oh how I missed him. No matter where I was...in Falmouth; at a concert; in my bed in Bristol. I was sure that nobody understood what I was going through. They weren't walking in my shoes.

Death was so final. Who needed this? This was a nightmare that wouldn't go away. It was devastating.

CHAPTER 14

~~~

My First Trip

During our life together, Victor and I were avid travelers. He was a million-miler and I was very close to that number. I actually achieved that level after his death. We loved to travel. Now I had to learn to travel alone.

I felt instinctively that I couldn't go anywhere in the world that we had traveled together because I suspected it would be too painful. I needed to discover places where we had not shared memories. I needed to create new ones.

Still, I had to make an effort to visit familiar places and friends in the United States.

So it was a welcome opportunity for me when a good friend, Irma, asked Susan and me to visit at a house she and Norman owned in Falmouth on Cape Cod. Yes, I had been there with Victor but I decided that I could not eliminate all the places and friends I had traveled to with him. Besides, it was time to try. These were good friends. Susan would be with me. So I took the plunge.

The morning I left on my trip I was scared, no make that terrified. Why? I had no idea. I guess because it was a first.

But, I reasoned, I'm going to a close friend. Someone I went to High School with; someone I shared a lifetime with. My daughter Susan will be with me. She was meeting me in Charlotte and we would travel the rest of the way together. Norman, whom I was very fond of was there, as was Irma's adult children who made a trip to Falmouth just to see me. There was no need to be nervous I told myself.

Nevertheless, I was.

Running through airports without him was a new experience. He seemed to be with me in memory every step of the way. I actually felt his presence in every corner of each airport. Strange and empty sensations accompanied me.

Overall, the trip went well. It gave me courage and a bit of strength to face the next hurdle. And it seemed to do a world of good for Susan, too.

But I did have one melt down after a perfect evening. We dined, along with another couple, at the Regatta, probably the most posh restaurant in Falmouth. Then we went to see Irma's daughter in concert. Elizabeth is an outstanding flautist with a marvelous reputation world-wide. She looked beautiful, played wonderfully and it was a great evening.

Following the performance, I hugged her, and congratulated her and felt honored that I had been there. But as soon as I sat in the car the tears started flowing. It was an avalanche of tears. I'm not sure where they came from or why. I cried the entire trip back to the house, said a quick good night and had a really good bawl after closing the door to my room.

I apologized the next morning to Norman, a renowned physician who told me, "You are doing great. You'll make it." He told me that I would have moments like that. Still, I was concerned that I had spoiled an otherwise lovely evening, but my friends seemed to understand.

Before we left for home, I told my daughter I would check out her room to make sure she hadn't forgotten anything. She had occupied the room I wouldn't stay in because I had shared it with Victor.

I looked in the closet. I looked under the bed. Everything was in order. Then I looked into each of the drawers.

In a bottom drawer I found Victor's bathing suit and swim suit cover. The cover he'd worn for years. We had wondered what had happened to it. It had obviously been left there on our last visit.

I was devastated. I froze and couldn't move. It was as if he was with me in that room. He was there and it seemed as if he was giving me a message. But he wasn't there. He would never be there again. It was eerie and sad.

That's how my daughter found me. Staring into a drawer.

I rushed out of the room and fled into the waiting limousine. I remember almost nothing of that trip to the airport.

CHAPTER 15

~⌒

Eating Out

One evening when I walked into our favorite restaurant, FATZ, the hostess pointed to the wall above the counter where one waited for the hostess to seat you.

There on the wall hung a memorial plaque with a picture of Victor in a tuxedo smiling at me.

The color photo had been reproduced from the memorial that appeared on Seaman Corporation's website. And the plaque simply read, "Victor Zager. We will miss you."

It was the managers who were responsible for that deed. This kind action totaled me and I completely lost it. I seemed to have more difficulty coping with nice gestures, rather than the reverse.

The aftermath of that kindness was that some patrons learned about Victor's death by seeing that plaque. Others, upon seeing it, would ask the staff about me and how I was doing.

One evening I had a call at dinner time from some casual friends who asked me join them at FATZ for dinner. They were probably the last people on earth I would have expected to call and invite me to dinner.

"He was always very nice to me," said the friend. His wife was in tears most of the dinner.

Interesting. Very interesting. They never asked me out again.

People's reaction to the news always fascinated me.

Some ignored me. I reasoned they didn't know what to say. A few women acted as if I was a threat to their marriage now that I was alone.

Still others befriended me and tried to help me. That's when I decided that God sends you people when you need them.

It would be more than a year later before I found out why I was being shunned by Allan. Allan, who sat by Victor's bedside and spoke at his funeral; Allan who had been a friend to both Victor and me for 50 years; I didn't hear from him at all.

His wife explained that he was mourning Victor's loss and somehow couldn't bring himself to face me. Nevertheless, it hurt.

Sometimes I wondered if I acted like the merry widow. I made sure I was dressed properly, wore makeup and a smile and cracked jokes. Who wanted to be with someone who was sad and depressed, I was thinking?

And I always listened to people's problems, offering what advise I could give. But it was an act. I would come home and tell myself, I've fooled them again.

One morning, two and a half months later, I awoke and said to myself, "I think I'm going to make it."

An hour later, I thought not.

Had fish and chips one evening and my mind went back to a London pub where Victor and I often enjoyed the fish and chips. It was located next door to the London hotel we stayed at. Sometimes we sat upstairs in the pub, sometimes downstairs while we drank lovely wine. Oh how I missed him and those days, especially at times like those when the memories were so real.

Everything I did or thought reminded me of Victor and everything I lost when he died.

One time at FATZ I was able to go an entire thirty minutes without focusing all my attention on Victor because I was consumed with the problems of others. I thought that was a good thing.

I always told people who served me my dinner to take their time, "I'm not in a rush," I would say. Where am I going I would wonder?

The people at that restaurant often said, "Makes me feel so good when I see you coming through the door. We all love you."

As I held court, dispensing advice at FATZ I heard some incredible stories. One waitress who was taking care of her grandfather as well as her two children talked to me about it; one was getting married the following day to a man she divorced twice; some of them had children out-of-wedlock; some were planning to marry the man who fathered their child; others not.

Everyone there seemed to have a problem. It reminded me of years ago when someone told me that everyone has problems, even a new born baby has problems. And it was nice that these people would come to me for help. It made me feel useful.

Of course some problems were more serious and threatening than others. Most servers were young with emotional baggage like love and problems connected with it. But there were those women whose babies were born while the father was in jail. Another's husband was dying.

But to me, one thing stood out as remarkable. These people always looked after me. They wouldn't let me leave FATZ without eating. They were so kind. I wonder if I would have survived without that place and those wonderful, caring people. They were my lifeline.

Each time I left FATZ, I would look at Victor's plaque and say a silent goodnight to him. And that would remind me of an old Jimmy Durante line: "Goodnight Mrs. Callabash, wherever you are."

CHAPTER 16

❧

My 75ᵀʰ Birthday

My first thought upon waking on my birthday was, it's been 60 years since I met him.

Happy, Happy birthday, to me!!!!!
HAPPY BIRTHDAY! *Allah manna sonem* (Yiddish for 'all my enemies') should have such a happy birthday!!

A friend sent two dozen of the most beautiful white roses sitting in an elegant vase. The family sent a gorgeous array of pink roses, carnations and assorted tiny yellow roses. The house was filled with beautiful, uplifting flowers. But I felt there weren't enough flowers in the world to help me 'celebrate' the occasion without my beloved.

I had calls from all over the country. Calls from overseas. Cards galore.

At FATZ, they tried every which way to cheer me up. There was a birthday card signed by the entire staff. They brought out a beautiful huge birthday cake with two candles, one had a two written on it; the other a one on it. That made for 21. Funny.

The staff came with the cake and one of the waitresses stood on the seat in the next booth and yelled at the customers, "It's Muriel's Birthday." Then they all sang happy birthday. The staff could not have been nicer. Nor tried harder to cheer me up. It was very touching.

But when I returned home I said to myself: As Victor would say, I'm spinning my wheels. What am I doing? Where am I going? So far, all I wanted to do was go through another day. It was hard to focus beyond one day. Even that was sometimes impossible to do. I tried to plan out what I would do the next few days. Still, I asked myself, WHERE AM I GOING????? I had no answer.

I remembered asking Victor, as he lay dying, if it was difficult. "No," he said, "this is not difficult." Well let me tell you, dying may not have been difficult. Living, for me, was difficult.

Just thinking about him, made me smile, and made me cry.

I tried to put that "other" life, the one with Victor behind me. It wasn't that
I couldn't see it, couldn't feel it couldn't remember it vividly. It was like remembering something in my childhood. I could see it and remember it, but it was over. It was in the past. The difference was that the life I shared with Victor left an emptiness and pain within me now that it was over. I wanted more. My childhood memories were at a different place. Those were simply memories. The memories of my life with Victor was my life.

Victor and I shared so much together. I felt as if I was drowning in a sea of memories.

One day I found a note in Victor's hand which said: "Rather than count on the days that I might have left, I'll make the most of each day I have left."

I have no idea when he wrote it. But that was exactly how we both lived. Making the most of each day together.

My 75th birthday, I was alone.

CHAPTER 17

Memories

Interesting how the memories would come charging through my brain at the oddest moments.

One day I was occupied with something else when I found myself in Seville, Spain, at a computer place we used to frequent. I could see before my eyes the owner, the place, the street, the discussions with the owner about the new trolley being installed outside on the main street, and the way the sun was shining. The entire scene was so vivid. It was as if I was living it at that moment. It was bizarre. Why think of this now? I asked myself.

Who knows? I answered.

I only knew that there was a flood of memories. A lifetime of memories that would suddenly appear. No regrets. Not even one. Just memories. A blessing of memories and glad to have them.

At those moments, I once again felt no one could know or understand the kind of relationship Victor and I had. Nor could anyone be as fortunate as I had been to have that relationship.

Just as suddenly a Paris café would pop into my mind. And the next minute I thought of how we, the children and I, used to tease him by calling him, Lucky Louis.

I remembered the time before we got married. We worried about his being sent to Korea. Would he be around for the wedding I had planned? His luck held out for that. Then I asked myself, is he still lucky Louis?

Often I thought about how our life together began. We were a little below what is known as humble beginnings. He was in the army; we lived with my parents; we had a baby within eleven months of our wedding.

Abruptly I would jump back to Spain: walking under the sheets in Seville, the ones with the Coca Cola logo on them, near our favorite restaurant. But it wasn't time for dinnertime so we went walking. It was twilight. We were walking toward the Ingles department store. Holding hands. Yes, we did a lot of that, even when he was dying.

There was so much to thank him for I hardly knew where to begin.

Vignettes of our life seemed to pop into my mind at all times. Songs and words would follow.

If that's all there is.....
Those were the days my friend.........
Que Sera Sera..........
One Day at a time...........
As he lay dying.

I remembered how he always said: stay out of hospitals and courtrooms. They dissipate your energy and you rarely get what you want.

It dawned on me one morning that this was the day we were to leave for Amsterdam and go on to Paris from there. That led my mind to focus on walking in Amsterdam – seeing the canals, shops, people eating outdoors, cafes on rooftops, beautiful. And as it always was with us whether we were on beaches or in cities, we held hands.

If I loved you, the song from the show "Carousel" that we had recently seen in a London revival jumped into my consciousness. In the theater during the rendition, he held my hand for the entire song. He was more of a romantic than anyone knew.

Waves of sorrow overcame me for the loss of a beautiful love.

Once again, I questioned whether anyone else had ever known a love like mine or a lover like mine.

And I felt as if the blood had been drained out of me.

Some thoughts repeatedly came to me. Over and over, the same thoughts. How I thanked him for a wonderful life as he lay dying. Told him how much I loved him. He told of his love for me. At least I had the chance to tell him how I felt.

At the hospital one time, he asked me to stay with him. Don't leave me, he said. I told him I would never leave him and begged him not to leave me.

He answered that we would always have Paris.

I never knew what he saw in me. He had so much more to offer than I did.

Victor was always kind to widows. He always made a special effort to look after them, to include them.

Shortly after he died a friend of his took me to lunch. I knew that was something Victor would have done.

My other life is over — abruptly- but it is over, I kept reminding myself. In order to move on I knew I had to create a new life, find out who this new me was, where I fit into the universe.

"I can't go back to the old…. Can't go around it can't go through it, have to go over it." I sang to myself. I had often offered that advice to others who told me of their misfortunes. It was time to take my own advice.

Victor made me strong. Whoever is better at something- should do it we decided. He was better at everything, I would tell him.

Although I recognized that it was better for him not to have suffered. Still, it seemed to me that time flew when he was in the hospital, and stayed still when he died.

He always had a great sense of humor and was ethical in every business and personal transaction. The world is a sad place without him.

56 years is a long time.

CHAPTER 18

~

Talking To Victor

Less than three months after Victor died I ran through the house yelling, Victor, where are you when I need you?

Luckily the house was so large and neighbors far enough away that no one heard me. I could scream and not worry about anyone having me locked up for disturbing the peace or worse.

Why did that thought cross my mind? Lexi, my teen-aged granddaughter, had a car accident. Totaled the car. Lost part of a finger. She needed surgery on the other two fingers. Still, she was very lucky because the car turned over three times down an embankment.

Those were the times I really needed to talk to Victor. To share crises.

I wondered what was it that possessed me to ask him as he was dying, if this was difficult? He said it wasn't. But what made me ask?

Of course Susan handled the whole hospital event with Lexi. David and Kitzi were in Boston, getting their son Mark off to Brandeis. Upon hearing the news Susan drove from Nashville to Jackson to be at the hospital with Lexi. Susan slept in Lexi's room the night before Lexi's surgery.

Kitzi returned the next day from Boston, David that evening. Beverly, the older granddaughter, flew from Texas. She and Jenny, another granddaughter, and Laura, a family friend, drove from Nashville to Jackson and helped Susan who had been signing papers and answering questions at the hospital.

And meanwhile I was, as usual, coping with the flooded memories I had with Victor. In my mind, during Lexi's crisis, Victor and I were walking in Paris. Five minutes later I was on a beach in Spain. There we were in San Diego going shopping for our New Year's Day Party.

HELP! I really felt my mind had completely left me. But my body went on.

Every day I thought, amazing, I made it through another day. How does one explain that feeling to anyone else?

Mentally I told Victor that I felt I was wasting time. What is the point of my existence, I asked him? Is that all there is? I didn't seem to have a purpose for living any more.

All I was trying to do was to live one day or one week at a time. Why? Who cared if I lived longer or not?

Who cared where I was going? Surely not me. Victor, I would cry out, I need you. You were my anchor. I'm just drifting now.

And no, I told him it is not getting easier.

Saw my gynecologist one day. He spoke with me and let me vent. He always talked with me for a while. That day was no different. He said some nice things about Victor and my relationship with Victor.

And when he examined my heart he said it was broken but it was still beating. Several times he said if I needed him to please not hesitate to call. It was a good visit, even if I was weepy.

Susan had her reconstructive surgery one morning. Another lovely day. At least Kitzi called to tell me that the surgery was over and Susan was doing fine. Jenny took Susan to the hospital and picked her up. Susan called me from Jenny's car to tell me she was okay and was pleased with the results.

It occurred to me that we really had a complete family. They were like one entity. Each pitched in for the others.

Susan became emotional. She was quite weepy. I think it was a delayed reaction. She said she thought she wanted to return to California on a permanent basis. We'll see.

At this juncture, I decided what should be written on Victor's tombstone. It was what David said to his father as his father was dying, "Victor Zager, A Righteous Man."

A friend thought I needed a project or hobby and I felt sure she was right. But I decided that I needed to drift for a while at that point in my life. Maybe later, I reasoned, when I could be more grounded. So I gave myself permission to do nothing. It seemed all right not to have an anchor at that point.

But I did ask Victor what would he do, if he was the one left without me? How would he handle this?

Like Lexi's accident and injuries or Susan's surgery, what would Victor have done? Dealing with those problems alone, was difficult. Not sharing those problems with him, wondering if I was handling those problems correctly, made every decision harder.

And the waves of memories still came crashing through more and more. Saw myself having lunch at the waterfront in Florida with Victor and Abbey. Now they were two dead bodies.

Still had that pain in the pit of my stomach. Will it ever go away, I wondered?

It seemed that each day I met at least one person who was unaware that Victor died. Each was devastated and I was consoling others again. A role I continued to play.

Then there were the people (mostly women) who seem to be avoiding me. I think they feared that widowhood was contagious.

Caught myself singing to Victor "Day by day, I'm growing more in love with you," one morning.

I decided that I would probably survive the Labor Day weekend as I expected Lynne and her family to come for a visit. Otherwise the three days would have been impossible.

The three months since Victor's death actually felt like three years. And I wondered, how many more years like that did I have to go through?

Dreamed one night that Victor and I were having sex. He said let's do it tomorrow and I said my father's favorite line, don't put off for tomorrow what you can do today. In the dream we had sex and I woke up at 3:00 a.m. and couldn't go back to sleep.

Sex and dying. It's interesting. Nobody talks about it. Sex, I mean, when you have lost a partner.

I was drifting. I had no plan, no future. I only had a past and what a wonderful past it was.

Spoke to a widow (at the Y) one morning. It was four years after she lost her husband and she still choked up and tears flowed as she talked about him. She must have had the kind of relationship (40 years) that I did. She said the pain in the stomach never goes away.

Wasting time. That's exactly what I was doing. I could find no reason for going on. No purpose to my life. No satisfaction with anything I did.

Just an inescapable feeling of dread that I would be this way for years and years to come.

I felt completely useless. I was not being productive. I was focused on one day at a time with no goal other than to eat and sleep and get through the agony.

But then I remembered that if life with Victor wasn't so wonderful this wouldn't be so miserable.

CHAPTER 19

Lifelines

One of my lifelines was FATZ, my neighborhood restaurant. Not too long after Victor died, I began to go there.

It wasn't easy going in there alone, but I forced myself to do so.

The first time I had to go into FATZ alone, a place Victor and I had frequented, I screwed up my courage, tried to suppress my emotions, put on some makeup and went.

But once inside, the managers, the wait staff, the hosts all greeted me, offered condolences and a lot of hugs. It buoyed me.

I began going there nightly. And they began to try to get me to eat. I had lost a good deal of weight and had no desire to eat but they were determined to see that I ate. They would think of different possibilities in order to whet my appetite.

One of the mangers asked me one day, "Is that all you're eating? Tomorrow, spaghetti for you."

A few days earlier I had been given a lecture about food disorders from a couple of good friends. Everyone seemed to be concerned about my health.

All the caring helped.

But I would sit at a table and have a flash of memory of being with Victor in some romantic place like our room overlooking the Arno in Florence.

One evening as I was sitting in FATZ, I was once again transported to Florence and remembered when I had my fortune told. On a dark corner in the Square a man sat behind a small table with a lit candle and cards on it.

The fortuneteller was named Eddie. Normally, I am awful at remembering names. But this man's name came to me immediately. I used to joke that was why I kept Victor around. He always knew people's names, and I relied on him to feed the names to me in social situations.

The night I had my fortune told in Florence, Eddie had looked at my palm, turned toward Victor and said, "We're going to have her around for a long, long time." Somehow sitting alone at FATZ, remembering those words made me cry. I didn't want to be around for a long, long time.

As I have mentioned before, during my nightly visits to FATZ I began to give advice, when asked, to many of the staff there. Some advice was for the lovelorn, for others I simply suggested how to live life or deal with illness or death. But giving advice made me feel useful and needed.

In connection with my journalism work, I had always said, scratch the surface and everyone has a story. It was true at FATZ. They had stories. The wonderful thing for me about FATZ was that I got involved with their problems, someone's cancer or cancer in their family, babies, deaths, money problems, school problems, etc. And while I was dealing with those problems, I had no time to think of my own.

Another night the owner of a car repair shop, JR, whom we befriended, came in. I hadn't heard from him and that bothered me because Victor had promised him Victor's prized old red Toyota.

I called that car a death trap and refused to go into it when Victor was alive. Now it sat on our driveway. Victor loved that old heap. And it was undoubtedly an antique. And I didn't want to part with it.

JR and his wife hadn't known about Victor's death until that night, they explained. They learned the news from the plaque on the wall at FATZ.

I told JR that I hadn't forgotten about Victor saying he could have the Toyota when Victor was through with it. It was just that I was enjoying seeing it sitting on the side of our garage. For some reason that car, which I hated when Victor was alive, gave me consolation seeing it sitting there, where Victor last parked it.

JR told me not to worry about it. When I want him to pick it up, he would. And in the meantime, if he or his wife could do anything for me, just call. Four and a half years later I actually did give him Victor's 1986 Toyota.

Under the circumstances I was doing extremely well. My situation was not something I felt I would "get over." As a matter of fact I would joke about it being a condition that you can't get over; you can't get under it; you have to go through it.

But I had a good support system in Bristol, and support from my family in Nashville and Jackson.

Some days every little thing took so much effort it seemed too much for me. Making a phone call or writing an email became a burden.

And I was still busy consoling others.

One day someone who worked at the airport came into FATZ. He told me, "My heart is breaking. I just love Victor. I use the present tense on purpose. His passing does not change that. Thank God he had time to say farewell to those he loved and those who loved him. He was one of the most wonderful people that I have encountered in my life. His old lady wasn't so bad, either. You may rest assured that I will keep in touch with you."

The reaction of the man who had taken care of cutting our lawn for years was that he was angry with me. "You shocked me," he said angrily. "I'm upset. You gave me a shock."

Part of the reason for what I was doing - keeping busy and going out to lunch with friends and going out to dinner at FATZ was to make sure my children didn't worry too much about me. I kept busy, involved myself with other people, and tried to give the appearance of moving on.

But I was really going on a day-to-day basis, trying to get the bare essentials taken care of; shopping, doing laundry, reading the mail and keeping social contacts. Making it through one more day.

It was all an illusion.

CHAPTER 20

Holy Days

Heading off to Nashville and the Jewish Holy Days, I was very nervous and dreaded it. I wondered how I would handle being in the synagogue that Victor and I attended each year, sitting in those same seats he and I sat in, this time with Susan at my side, and Victor no longer on this earth.

How would I handle the prayers and the praying? It had always been a difficult time of year for me. The introspection, the thinking of the past year and what it had brought. And the prayer that loomed so large in my mind was the one that asks: Who will live and who will die, who will fall ill and who will recover?

Said during the Days of Awe that prayer reads: On Rosh Hashanah will be inscribed and on Yom Kippur will be sealed; how many will pass from the earth and how many will be created; who will live and who will die; who will die at his predestined time and who before his time; who by water and who by fire, who by sword, who by beast, who by famine, who by thirst, who by storm, who by plague, who by strangulation, and who by stoning. Who will rest and who will wander, who will live in harmony and who will be harried, who will enjoy tranquility and who will suffer, who will be impoverished and who will be enriched, who will be degraded and who will be exalted.

For years I took stock of the past year and wondered who would survive the following year. Sitting in the synagogue during those Days Of Awe was rough. Some in the congregation would ask where Victor was. One congregant said he missed Victor's singing voice. Another missed the beautiful way my husband prayed. Still others missed him and his congenial manner.

Of course I cried. Bitter tears. We had prayed together for more than 50 years. How could I not?

CHAPTER 21

~~⌒

Solo To Boston

As I left on my trip to Boston to attend the twice-yearly Emerson College Board of Overseers meeting I was terrified. I now knew I could handle traveling to Boston or anywhere by myself. So why was I so stressed? Why did I feel nervous? Maybe it was because I was going to a place I always traveled to with Victor.

At the airport I found myself shaking. I was nervous and teary-eyed. It didn't help my emotions when one of the security guards asked, "Isn't your husband going on this trip with you?" Here we go again, I thought and proceeded to console her.

I thought I was okay; thought I could handle whatever came my way; thought I had a new direction; thought I could go it alone; but on the plane my stomach pain returned with a vengeance. I remembered that Victor always said a prayer before take-off and landing. So I did that in his memory. A first for me.

I tried desperately not to cry in public. Sometimes I even succeeded. When will it truly end? I wondered. My answer? Never.

At the social dinner the night before the Emerson Board meeting there were lots of hugs; there were some of the attendees who didn't know about Victor dying; others wanted to know how I was doing.

This dinner was an event that Victor always attended with me. So I was not only nervous but a bit emotional as well. Emerson's president came over to my table to tell me how much she appreciated my coming to the meeting and to say how much she admired Victor and was thankful for all he did. Luckily I am a good actress.

And I learned something. I learned that by being on the Board of Overseers at Emerson, I could be of use to the students and the board. Once again I found that I could be useful; I had resources. The board and the students made me feel as if I was important to Emerson. The accolades at the dinner and reception; the gift they bestowed on me; the adoration of the students; the introductions; all made me feel that maybe my life did have some meaning.

I was staying at a bed and breakfast called The College Club. It was a most unusual place, located in Boston's historic Back Bay area. The College Club of Boston was the oldest women's college club in America. It was located on Commonwealth Avenue in a Victorian brownstone.

My room could have doubled for a banquet hall. The room had high ceilings and was furnished magnificently. Fireplace, desks, large king bed, oriental rugs and enough room for a dance floor. It had everything. The only thing missing was Victor.

The B & B also had a very interesting set-up for breakfast and a coffee machine that could be used all day.

That night I dreamed I told Victor about the varieties of cereal at The College Club. I think he would have liked the place.

My purpose for the trip was twofold. Besides the meeting, I was going to spend a weekend with Mark, my grandson, who was a freshman at Brandeis University. I was planning to show him around Emerson, go to the science museum, eat at fun restaurants and basically share a lovely weekend.

What helped me get through those few days was the fact that Mark joined me on Friday evening after my meeting. He enjoyed coming to the College Club and seeing my room.

Mark and I had dinner with some friends of mine and after dinner Mark left. When I was back in my room, alone, I found myself, once again, talking to Victor. So much I want to tell you, I said. One thing in particular I wanted him to know was that our friend said what a nice young man Mark is.

And Mark was so sweet. He held my hand as we walked. Did he remember that I once I told him that Victor and I held hands as we walked through the world? I wasn't sure. It didn't matter. He lifted up my spirits at that moment. And I told him so.

While taking a walking tour of Boston the next day, I thought about Mark's birth and the look on his father's (David, our son) face.

Mark told me that most kids say yuk, I have to go visit my grandma, but he looks forward to seeing me. That's because I'm not like most grand-mothers, I argued. He quickly agreed that I'm not a normal grandma.

We laughed a lot, Mark and I. And that was what I missed the most traveling without Victor. And that brought Paris, to mind, once again. Our room in Paris, laughter, shopping, museums and decisions made together. What to do today, was always discussed at breakfast.

I had not as yet gotten used to being accountable only to myself.

Mark and I spent the day together. Showing Mark around Boston gave me a wonderful feeling.

Still, at the airport when I walked into the Delta Club Lounge, the flood of memories from seven months earlier when Victor and I were together in this same lounge hit me. It seemed like a lifetime ago.

It was a lifetime ago.

Having so far survived the trip, I sat in the lounge and came to the con-clusion that I might some day be all right. Never will my life be like it was,

I told myself, but I think I'll make it. Interestingly enough that thought made me feel a bit guilty. As if surviving was selfish.

On the flight home many thoughts came to mind. Even in crowds, on planes that were full of people, the realization that I was without Victor engulfed me.

Deep in thought about the zillion flights we took together. I was startled when the man in the seat next to mine asked, "Are you traveling alone?" He meant no harm and I knew it was an innocent question. But it was like a knife in my heart. My new life, my whole existence could be summed up in the words, I am traveling alone.

So I ordered a glass of wine on the plane and thought of Victor who would order some wine and say he didn't want his wife to drink alone. Then I would drink my wine, he would take a sip of his and I would finish the rest of his glass. That thought made me smile.

I also thought about the fact that I had a wonderful day with Mark. I began to think that maybe I was getting better. Almost as soon as that thought entered my mind, I went into a deep depression.

I felt melancholy again, sad, depressed. And I kept saying to myself, God how I miss him.

My next thought was that I was back again to thinking my life was over.

On the plane coming back someone opened a paper bag and took out a sandwich. That reminded me of the many times we bought a sandwich at Finegele, a bagel shop in Boston. We would order bagels to take home the day before and pick them up on our way to the airport.

We would have a bagel and light cream cheese for breakfast while they packaged our order. We purchased two sandwiches of Swiss cheese, tomato and honey mustard on sesame bagels to take on the plane. Victor would supervise the sandwich creation. We'd pack up the bagels in plastic bags, stuff them into suitcases, and he'd carry our sandwiches in his briefcase.

Later, we'd eat on the plane while drinking a glass of wine and enjoying that delicious sandwich. I could almost taste it. Thinking of those days my throat closed up and my eyes were filled with tears.

But I did make the trip. And people complimented me because I was doing so well. Once again I felt was a sense that I had fooled them again. I knew I no longer had my anchor. Victor was my anchor.

My ride home from the airport was unusual because I had never shared the limo with anyone else. But this time I was asked if I minded sharing it because the man needing a ride lived a few doors down from my house,

It turned out the owner of the limo service had just told him about Victor. Here was another one to comfort. There seemed to be no end to consoling people on the loss of Victor.

And even though it was months later, when I arrived at home, I found two condolence letters from people who just heard the news.

CHAPTER 22

Six Months Later

Six months had passed.

If this was all there was and this was the way the rest of my life was going to be, I thought, at least I had good friends and the people at FATZ.

Memories flooded over me more often now it seemed. Scenes of our time together in different places on the globe played out in my mind vividly and in color.

It was so real I could almost reach out and touch it.

London was particularly strong at that point. So was San Diego. Pumpkin waffles came to mind. On our last visit to San Diego, last December, Victor, the man I never saw order, no less eat, waffles ordered pumpkin waffles.

It was probably the time of year that got to me. We always went to San Diego in December; went to London in January.

And the dreams kept coming. He was so alive in my dreams, I hated to wake up. One dream found me offering him my wool blanket that was covering me. I'm not cold and you are I said. Once again we held hands. So alive, but only in my dreams.

Had a night with the Ya Ya's. They were a group of very interesting women who went to dinner once a month. When Victor was alive, I occasionally joined them because more often than not I wanted to spend my evenings with Victor.

Being out with a group of eclectic women and making it through dinner that night, once again gave me hope that I could make it. Next day my stomach pain returned.

My hairdresser told me of a program she saw dealing with death where the dead got in touch with the living in two ways, through dreams and through smell. I did dream of Victor often and one time I thought I could detect his essence on my sheet. But I didn't believe that the dead could contact the living. I could not accept the idea that one can somehow reach those who have left this world.

The dead are dead.

One morning I woke and I realized that I was beginning to plan a future: a trip a month at least until May. That was a first. Until then, I couldn't even think in those terms. It gave me a reason to go on living at least until May.

Dick Seaman, the president of Seaman Corporation where Victor was a consultant for many years, invited me to a dedication at the Industrial Park in Bristol. The invite included dinner at the Troutdale Restaurant that evening. I felt both happy and sad about the invitations.

The dedication turned out to be quite an event. Dick, Judy, his wife, two of their adult children, and the board members from Ohio were there.

One man from the plant reminded me that we used to have picnics at the farm we owned years ago when the man worked for Incopa. That was the original plant that opened years ago in the Industrial Park. It was the reason Victor and I moved to Bristol.

The plant manager's wife and friend picked me up and drove me to the plant. There, I was ushered to a seat as if I was attending a wedding of a close relative.

A printed program was at my seat and I followed along, as did all the local dignitaries: Mayor, senators, aldermen, etc. After the ribbon cutting, that was the last item on the program, Dick asked the audience if he could have a few more minutes. He called me up to the platform.

Dick began by explaining Victor's vital roll in the company and how Dick had spent a year negotiating the sale of the plant to his family. He said he learned a lot about negotiations from Victor.

He went on to say that he had showed Victor through the plant and it's expansion a few weeks before Victor died and Dick thought it was the only time he found Victor speechless.

Then Dick read from a framed plaque that he presented to me. It held Victor's smiling photo and was a Seaman Board proclamation which had been posted on their website.

I managed to be stoic throughout that ceremony. Even toured the facility with Dick and praised the growth of the plant explaining my understanding Victor's being speechless. The company had done a beautiful job of expansion.

After the tour, I was driven home, opened the door, turned off the alarm and screamed the way I did when I came home to pack for our trip to Nashville when Victor was dying.

My crying lasted for a good part of the rest of the day.

That evening I was picked up and taken to the reception. The last time I had been to a reception in that private room was with Victor at another Seaman dedication two years earlier.

Somehow I made it through the evening but I'm not sure I know how I did it.

Uncontrollable screaming. Primal scream was what Barbara called it. She was still helping me through the journey.

I suppose I screamed because I was so tired of being brave. When I was alone, I could cry. I could let go of my pent up emotions.

People kept telling me how wonderful I was and how marvelous I looked. But it was always best if people didn't ask how I felt. The mask I wore in public was not how I felt at all.

I kept remembering that Victor told me dying wasn't difficult. There was no question in my mind that living was difficult.

How could I explain to others why I was so unbearably miserable? I asked myself why I quite literally cried into my wine?

My answer was: it's Vic, it's Vic, it's Vic. And there were not enough bottles of wine or tears in this world to alleviate my suffering. The good thing about screaming, I thought, was that nobody heard me.

CHAPTER 23

First Pleasure Trip

I kept explaining to everyone that my daughter needed a vacation and that was why I was going. Maybe I needed one as well, but could not seem to admit it. The truth was that I felt guilty about taking a pleasure trip. Didn't know why, but I was guilty. Furthermore, as with all firsts, I was frightened.

Questions kept running through my head: Where am I going? I don't know. Why am I going? Because I have no choice.

On the night before I left I went through the same thing I went through before I left for Boston. It made me realize that it doesn't seem to get easier.

I kept telling myself, the trip would be great; it would be wonderful. But what I really thought was: thank goodness, it will soon be over.

November 1st was one of the dates that would be coming up during our trip. I tried not to think about the surprise 80th birthday party for Victor the family had planned and was to be held on that date. Nevertheless, I couldn't stop thinking about what might have been.

At the airport, once again, another security guard asked, where's your other half?

In the Caymans, Victor was with me every inch of the way. There was no escape.

The room reminded me of the room I shared with Victor at Guadalmar, in Spain. The pool reminded me of the pool at Guadalmar.

The walk on the beach reminded me of the beach at Guadalmar.

When it rained it reminded me of Spain, or of Italy - of walking in Milan in the rain.

The coffee shop in the Caymans reminded me of the coffee shop in Frankfurt – the small one opposite the college.

Drinks at the Ritz Carlton Hotel in the Caymans reminded me of drinks Victor and I had at the Ritz Carlton in Boston our last time there together.

When I realized I had not cried for a while, guilty tears appeared. I felt guilty when I found myself enjoying something. And I was also melancholy. Maybe I did need that respite, after all.

Being away from home made me realize that maybe there was a tomorrow. Although he was always was with me wherever I went, the lessening of the intensity of his presence seemed to give me hope that things might eventually get better.

Victor's birthday a few days later was not easy – but easier, I was sure, than if I stayed at home, by myself. I kept thinking of him, talking to him in my mind telling him, 'You would have turned 80. We would have had a wonderful time. You didn't. We didn't.

Flying back the yearning and the pain returned full blast. Interestingly, I didn't have that strong pain in the pit of my stomach while on the trip. While on the trip, although that awful pain that surfaced when he died had never left me, it was less severe.

And when I returned home, it seemed to me that I was even weepier than when I left. But I knew it was easier spending his birthday away. And it was certainly better to be with Susan and far away from his big 80th surprise birthday party that never was.

CHAPTER 24

Pain

Everything seemed to increase that awful pain in the pit of my stomach. The pain never left me; only sometimes it was worse.

One day I found a note in Victor's handwriting. I think it was written when he suffered so badly that Memorial Day weekend. It said:

Something to manage the pain that is not detrimental to my kidney. Relieve the pain. Fluid in my belly. 500 (liters?)
Terrible discomfort. I have to see the doctor today.

Naturally that caused MY pain to increase. Although seeing anything in his handwriting unnerved me.

What helped me through the next few weeks was my support system. Although I'm not sure I realized I had such a good group of friends before Victor's death, during the long days and nights alone made me realize that they were there for me. I'm not sure I would have survived without these caring people.

Barbara met me weekly and listened to my sorrows. She had always been there for me but for those many miserable days, weeks and months she was a breath of sunshine.

What was most interesting for me was that she said she was learning from me. According to her, I seemed to be a good role model for a grieving widow. I did not grieve in public, made sure I dressed appropriately and laughed when in the company of others. Even I recognized that laughter would not only get me through this difficult time, but would also make people more comfortable when they were with me. To me that meant they would not mind my company. And, heaven knows I needed to be with people.

Rita and Murray, good friends drove forty minutes each way from Jonesboro once a week after work to take me to dinner. Rita and Murray's company, their dedication and their warmth sustained me.

And there were several others who took me to lunch, took me to dinner, invited me to go to the movies with them, saw to it that when I was with them I could be comforted and could be reassured.

On the other hand, there were those whom I never heard from. That hurt. People I had thought were close friends stopped calling. Cut me off. I found it difficult to understand.

I'm talking about couples Victor and I had known for years. Still others treated me as if I had the plague. That hurt, too.

And then there were those whom I had never been particularly close with who came forward and became really good friends. They watched over me and saw to it that I was made to feel part of their lives. Those people uplifted my spirits. That's when I knew that God sends you people when you need them

As I said before, FATZ was a lifeline. The management and staff there took me under their wings and offered me their hearts. They made sure I ate; made sure I was not alone when I sat there; and allowed me to dispense advice. They came to me with their problems and I tried not only to listen to them but to help them though their problems. That made me feel useful and allowed me to contribute something in return for their caring.

It also afforded me the will to leave the house and be with people, rather than to stay home and hibernate. Even though there were times when I thought I wanted to just curl up and hide from the world, this sense of purpose drew me out- not only of my house, but of myself.

CHAPTER 25

November 25, 2008 – Wedding Anniversary

The night before at what would have been our 57th wedding anniversary, I had an around the world mental trip with Victor at my side. We would be in Paris, one minute, San Diego, the next.

I remembered how often I would tease him about his doing everything better than I did. It was no joke. But I wondered if he would be handling my loss better than I was handling the loss of him.

As I was sipping wine at the FATZ bar waiting for a table to open, a man walked in and for a split second, I thought it was Victor. It was even less than a split second. Now I was positive I had lost my mind.

The man had a similar build and walk. Maybe it was wishful thinking that this nightmare was just that- a nightmare. As if Victor could just walk in; like his death never happened. It was a weird feeling. I started crying and that was a real first. I had been extremely careful to never cry in public. Now I couldn't stop.

To put it mildly, this was a really hard journey I was on. And there seemed to be no relief. This will be my life forever, I thought.

With Thanksgiving coming the next day and going to Nashville to be with the family to celebrate Thanksgiving (and our anniversary) my emotions were raw. Thanksgiving had always been a special time for the family.

But the next day, there I was at the airport once again. This time the ticket agent, the TSA agents, the boarding personnel, each in his turn hugged me and said they are praying for me. Special prayers were offered when I told them it was my anniversary. Special, they said, because of the occasion, but they said they always had me in their prayers.

One TSA Agent, whom we were very close with, asked me if I thought that Victor realized he was dying. Thinking it was an unusual question I asked why? Then she explained.

The last time she saw Victor and me at the airport was a couple of weeks before his death. Victor had told her she was beautiful inside and outside and that she should take care of her family.

At that point, she was confused and turned to the agent at her side and said, "What was that all about? I'll see him again."

But of course she never did.

It made her wonder if Victor knew he would not be living much longer.

Another TSA agent called me back to the table to tell me that Victor is always with me looking out for me.

Still, the person who touched me the most that day was the agent who said, "You two were so close, anyone could see that."

There seemed to be longer stretches between the pains in my stomach. But on that Thanksgiving Day the pain returned full force.

Feeling lousy, was putting it mildly.

It was difficult walking into David's house and seeing the beautiful table Kitzi set. Victor would have rushed for his camera. He always did. I just choked up. There were several choked up moments during that weekend. But I survived and in the end, the holiday turned out better than I expected.

David, Susan and I visited the cemetery where Victor was buried in order to see what kind of stone had been placed on other graves. Time for ordering a stone for Victor's grave was fast approaching. We wanted to see the type of stones that were in that cemetery and we had to determine what words were to be written on Victor's.

Besides, what better place to celebrate our anniversary than at the foot of his grave, I thought?

At first David was reluctant to go to the cemetery. He explained that the Temple was closed and we wouldn't be able to get on the cemetery. I told him that a cemetery is always open. Besides, I felt I HAD to go. David didn't understand how important this was for me. Nor did he realize all the arrangements that went into an unveiling. He had never needed to deal with this before. It was not just the placing of the stone. Preparations need to be made.

I couldn't sleep the night before we went. When I woke I called David early the morning after Thanksgiving. He was in his car returning from taking Bev, Steve and great-grandchild Zach to the airport. David agreed to take me to the cemetery but he warned me, once again, that the Temple would be closed and possibly the cemetery.

To be sure, he stopped at the Temple on his way home and discovered that, as I had said, a cemetery is never closed. People like to visit whenever they can and so the doors and fence to a cemetery are never closed. So Susan, David and I went.

We looked over the stones on the graves. I said I didn't want to go over to Victor's grave. No sooner had I said I didn't want to go there than I ran to Victor's grave.

There was a small marker in the ground, signifying nothing. I said a quick prayer and left. It was enough. David and Susan must have thought their mother was completely nuts.

The following day was the worst day I'd had in a long time. I seemed lonelier than ever and felt weepy eyed and missed my husband beyond words.

Victor was always alive in my dreams. In my dream that night I told him that I didn't miss sex while he was gone but now that he was back we'd have sex on the weekend.

My anniversary sex, I called it.

When I woke I thought, my children were probably right if they thought I was loosing my mind.

Days later when I was back in Bristol, a man called. I had sat next to him on the plane going to Nashville for Thanksgiving. He called me from Brussels because he knew from our onboard conversation that Brussels was my "least favorite" city. We had joked about that on the trip.

He said he was thinking about me all through the holiday and wondered how I made out. Wanted me to be sure to keep him on my monthly column mailing list.

I felt it was very compassionate of him to call and to remember me. You never knew where you would find people who were kind and caring. Those people helped me through some of my hardest times.

CHAPTER 26

~~~

More Dreams

What a dream.

Victor was alive. I was with Victor, David and Susan. Victor was try-ing to get his frequent flyer miles. He had just come from some doctor because he had a bandage over his left chest (I think it was over his heart but I couldn't see it because he was wearing a shirt) and he didn't want to be hugged because he was sore.

I explained that we thought he was dead and that was why I had tried to get his frequent flyer numbers. He looked hurt. I told him I could prove that he was dead. We had a death certificate, several in fact. I told him that even the people at the frequent flyer desk thought he was dead.

And then I kissed and kissed him on his face. But he reminded me not to hug him because it hurt. I was so very glad he wasn't dead.

Another dream.

This time I was at an airport and Victor was there with me. I was using some of his 652,000 frequent flier miles and arguing with the clerk for a free taxi ride to the airport.

Victor was holding my ticket and he said he would get me a free ride. I asked him if the frequent flier mile ticket was a fraud because he was alive.

One more.

This time I asked Victor, "As long as you're here, do I have to pay taxes on the money that you left me in the safety deposit box?"

I asked him if he was alive. I answered myself that he couldn't be doing all the things he does in my dreams if he wasn't. He gave me a marvelous, warm hug that I could actually feel. And it felt so very good.

"Good Night Sweet Prince" came to mind when I awoke. It's the last line in a biography about John Barrymore. I wrote a synopsis of it in Jr. High School, so many years ago.

In another dream I was with two friends who are medical physicians and are married to each other.

I was on a plane alone. We landed. Through the window I saw both doctors. I said, "Oh no."

The woman next to me asked, "What's the matter?" I answered, "Nothing".

My doctor friends were fighting their way through the crowd of people who were trying to exit the plane. I was in the back. I tried to fight my way through in order to get to my friends. They had medical equipment with them and I told them I didn't need the equipment.

Next thing I knew, all three of us were in their car and I was stretched out in the back seat. She was driving very slowly. I fell asleep telling them all I needed to do was to sleep. I am just tired, I told them. But she insisted that she was going to go to Walgreens East. We hit several bumps in the road. All I kept thinking of was how very tired I was.

Victor and I were riding on a bus somewhere in England in still another dream. Although I was not sure if it was in London, we had tickets to something. I think it was a concert that was to start at 6:00 p.m. We were not sitting together on that bus. We were separated. I recognized where we had to get off. And so I left the bus. Victor didn't.

I thought he must have fallen asleep and I started to panic.

Should I follow the bus? Take a taxi to the end of the line and meet him there? Go to the pub we passed when on the bus on the other street and wait for him there? I noticed that the pub looked more like a warehouse than a pub.

All of a sudden I seemed to know what to do. I'll call him on his cell phone, I thought. That's what they're for I told myself. But before I could do that I woke up.

In yet another dream, I was making coffee in our house in North Bellmore, N.Y. We used to live in that house before moving to Tennessee many, many years ago. Victor was at the kitchen table in that house. Someone else was in the room. It seemed to me it was our youngest daughter, but I wasn't sure. Nevertheless Victor asked her to mail something for him. I added that I had something to mail, also.

I turned to Victor and explained that I had done a lot while he was away, and now I needed to turn everything back over to him just like I used to do when he was traveling and the children were little.

I had very weird dreams during that Cayman trip Susan and I made after Victor died.

In one dream, I was putting on a show in High School. Adults, part of a Christian group, were there and so was my son, David. One woman in a white hat walked out –insulted. The minister had a briefcase where some ink was dripping inside of it and I was trying to mop it up with a tissue.

Someone I knew years ago was in charge. She was angry with me. David claimed that people were bored, and said we had to end the show. I announced that the end was coming and told everyone to prepare for the finale.

There was a really professional Santa Claus and elves entertaining the crowd who loved them. An older woman declared that she and Santa Claus had just gotten married.

In another Cayman dream Victor and I went into a hotel that was built peculiarly into the side of a mountain. We couldn't find where the check-in was. Couldn't find the floor. People were cleaning in the crooked hall.

The restaurant resembled a place we went to long ago in New York. In the dream we were in the restaurant and I was checking the prices on the menu. Victor asked what I was doing. Told him I was checking the prices. I told him I didn't expect to stay because it was pricey. But he seemed to have known that.

I told him I knew why we were there. It was because he wanted to have sex. I said we could have had sex at home. And there's a swimming pool at the YMCA. There was no reason to stay at the hotel, or to be in the restaurant. But he decided to stay at the hotel and to eat at the restaurant, anyway.

While I was looking for a large plate to put the food on, the waitress told me that the plates were almost ready. She suggested I go into the kitchen to get one. I wanted to know why I should go into the kitchen when I had a small plate that would be fine to taste the veggies and spaghetti dish. However, there was a woman eating right out of the serving dish. I noticed that Victor had a large plate but he suddenly decided to leave.

In the parking lot a woman was driving very fast and scraped our car. She came running out of her car, blaming Victor.

She's a liar and a cheat I told the several other women who had gathered around the cars. Everyone asked why anyone should believe me. They claimed they did not have to believe me.

I answered them. I told them that I knew each of them was a friend of the woman in the accident. One woman said that they were all women of parodies. That made me decide that the woman who caused the accident was afraid to tell her husband about it and that was why she blamed us.

After coming home from the Caymans, one night I dreamt that it was raining through the ceiling inside my house. It seemed the house was in need of repair. Part of the ceiling fell into my hand – one large complete piece. I held onto it thinking maybe we can re-attach it.

I turned to Victor who once again was alive in my dream and told him we needed to do a few things around the house. We needed a paint job, and other things as well, because the house was getting seedy.

Victor agreed. He said we have to do it. But he added that the reason we had decided to do some work around the house was because of something that happened earlier. He didn't elaborate.

One morning, more than a year after he died, I was startled awake by his voice shouting my name.

Explanation? I have none.

CHAPTER 27

Interpretation???

Shortly after I had that series of dreams, Rabbi Adam Frank, the Rabbi of the Jerusalem Synagogue where we were life members wrote in the Synagogue Newsletter:

Parashat Miketz

"In Parsha, Miketz, Joseph's dream interpretation takes center stage. A rationalist has the tendency to dismiss the significance of dreams. Others are willing to acknowledge that dreams have significance but fear dream interpretation lest the true message of the dream be misconstrued.

"There are the schools of psychological thought which claim that dreams are manifestations of the human subconscious which tell more about the dreamer than even her waking hours.

"What is a Jewish take on dreams? The Talmud (B.T. Brachot 55a) teaches that 'an unanalyzed dream is like an unopened letter' – until it is read, its contents never truly exist for the recipient.

"Rashi interprets this to indicate that the meaning of a dream follows its interpretation. But, perhaps it is more accurate to say that the message and meaning of a dream are real and informative and of consequence.

"Also, a dream that is ignored does not change its truth; it merely reinforces the recipient's lack of awareness. Thankfully, in this Torah portion the Pharaoh has the wisdom to desire the comprehension of his dreams."

I found it interesting that Rabbi Frank's interpretation of dreams came shortly after my series of dreams and Rabbi Frank's words led me feel that my dreams had meaning after all.

If I could just interpret them, I thought, it might help.

So my interpretation was that I was subconsciously wishing Victor was back with me, and alive, despite what I knew to be the truth. It was my wish that we would travel together again and life would go on as before.

Simple interpretation, but at that moment in time it made sense and gave me solace.

CHAPTER 28

⌁

Discoveries

When I least expected it, things turned up.

I had been into the safe deposit box several times after Victor died, but somehow I had not seen it. One day I discovered, inside an envelope addressed to me, a note written, in Victor's hand.

On the envelope was written: FOR MURIEL: open after my death.

How I missed it earlier I cannot say, but inside the envelope there was some important papers and this note:

Dear Muriel:

We know not the hour that God will call - But this we know- All things come to an end and we sleep in the dust till eternity -

So say that of me.

My life has been good, especially the years with you and the children and as I always told Lynne, if you want me, just think of me and I'll be there.

Farewell, until we meet again.

Victor

After I stopped crying, I once again reminisced about how our life together began. So many thoughts repeated in my mind, again and again.

He was a blind date for a friend of mine; I was a blind date for a friend of his.

I used to joke that his friend wasn't very bright, nor was he very good looking whereas Victor was everything his friend was not.

Victor asked me to dance. We did and I gave him my phone number. I was 15 years old.

For years I claimed that when we married we actually were a little below what is known as humble beginnings.

Victor was in the army so we moved in with my parents. I insisted on having a big wedding because I maintained we would have money some day but I could only have a wedding once.

His bank account was depleted before that wedding because Victor bought me a beautiful diamond engagement ring and a diamond wedding ring, which I wore for 56 years. I still wear them.

Victor told me that the reason he spent all his savings on that jewelry was because he didn't know if he would ever be able to afford to buy me anything like that in the future. He had accumulated those funds by working from the age of 12.

Many years later we saw his friend, my blind date. He was a brilliant scientist and a very handsome man. Obviously when I met Victor, I saw only Victor.

Once again, I was transported back to Seville and that computer place we frequented. I could mentally float back to the store where Victor would talk with the owner as I retrieved email messages. The scene unfolded vividly.

On that remembered day in Seville Victor and the owner had a discussion about the trolley that ran through the heart of Seville and had been completed a few days earlier. I could see the train running, the sun shining on its roof, directly outside the store.

Just as suddenly, a Paris café we liked popped into my mind. The Depart. And there we were. People watching as we drank wine and talked.

My mind flew back to Spain and I saw us walking under the Coca Cola sheets in Seville. We were walking near our favorite restaurant but it was not dinnertime yet.

Twilight. We were going toward the Ingles department store. Holding hands. We did a lot of that, I thought, even when he was dying. Wonderful memories

As I sat in the cubbyhole in the bank, fingering Victor's note those memories came charging through my mind. A flood of memories. A lifetime of memories. No one could know the kind of relationship we had, I told myself. No one else could be that fortunate, I realized.

There was so much to thank him for I hardly knew where to begin. I was truly grateful for all the love I had been given. But that note told me, that he was reaching out to me, knowing how difficult this would be. He was once again, trying to hold my hand to get me through it.

I left the bank, feeling that Victor, who was a blessing to me, would always be with me on some level.

CHAPTER 29

Christmas

It was Christmas Eve and I transported myself to Anthony's on the pier in San Diego where we spent many a Christmas Eve. I could see it all so clearly. It was so beautiful. The water was shining and the lights from a passing boat made it look so peaceful as we sat at a window table sipping wine with our meal and just enjoying the quiet.

Although it was the same holiday that Victor and I shared in San Diego, I was at FATZ that night and I realized that the water at the restaurant in San Diego was the remembrance, FATZ was the reality.

I thought of the words to a song: If that's all there is then let's keep dancing.

Then I noticed a man around 55 years of age, sitting at the table across from mine. He kept looking at me. Trying to steal glances every few minutes for at least half an hour.

Here I was, wondering who he might be, another human being eating alone on Christmas Eve. I knew he was trying to figure out who I was. I would have loved to tell him, I'm the mystery woman in the play THE WOMAN IN BLACK. And then I realized I was dressed all in black. I found that amusing.

In my mind I flashed back again: it was night and Victor and I were walking in San Diego near the port. Walking holding hands, loving one another; walking past the familiar places; the shopping area; past the naval yard to Anthony's Restaurant on the water; watching the boats gliding in the darkness; enjoying just being together.

Sitting at FATZ on Christmas Eve, I worked out in my head how I was going to survive another weekend. Somehow, I did.

And then it was Christmas day and I had an email from cousins in San Diego remembering all the, "lovely Christmas days spent with you and Victor."

Another one came from Ruby, one of my Palestinian daughters:
"Hi, Just to let you know that I am thinking of you during the holidays.
"I feel God blessed me by knowing you and Victor. I always think of the things that he used to teach me. You will be always in my heart and mind.
Love you.
Ruby"

That night I wished, once again, he had taken me with him. What was the point in my going on?
It was a long, hard, difficult unproductive day.

And my mind kept reliving all the thoughts of the past. Random thoughts of places we shared and my life without him. He left me with all of this, the house, the collections of things, the memories. But the bottom line was that he left me without HIM.

I asked God to help me through this life that I hated but had no choice but to live. And I talked to myself a lot.

A flood of memories enfolded in my mind's screen. I talked to Victor. Asked him if he remembered walking in Malaga, Spain, at the oldest wine shop there. 'Bring your old bottles, we fill it from kegs,' the sign read.

We enjoyed a glass of wine and then we walked around the corner to the church. It suddenly started to rain.

Do you remember, I asked out loud to an empty house? Of course he remembers, I answered myself. Then I wondered does he now have the capacity to remember?

Talking to myself, and seeing images of the past made me, once again, wonder if I was losing my mind. Sometimes I thought I was, and was quite convinced that I resembled the Mad Woman of Chaillot.

Christmas Day, the year before, Victor and I were in a quiet romantic corner at the upper level of a restaurant in a wooden House overlooking a blue/ black sea in San Diego.

This year even Hanukah was hard for me. Why was that? It was never a really important holiday to us. Yes, we lit candles, said the prayers, sang the songs. Why did it now feel so important? My answer to me: Without him everything is important.

Looking at some of the things we bought in different places in the world; holding the package of Spanish almonds (almondos he called them); putting away the Hanukah menorahs; wondering what life will be like when I take out the Hanukah candles next year. All I could think of was that nothing was the same without him.

There was no one around to share our shortcuts: a few words that spoke volumes; Looks that told stories.

Dark nights in London came to mind, empty streets, holding gloved hands, walking past the restaurant called, Slug In The Lettuce, on our way back to the hotel.

And thinking of my good Israeli friend Hettie who years ago told me that one of you pays a price when you have such a special relationship. Hettie who was still paying the price in her nineties. And me, paying the price now.

CHAPTER 30

 ❧

Holidays

Woke one morning between Christmas and the New Year at 4:00 a.m. and decided it was going to be a wonderful day. Went to the gym, and while exercising on one of the machines, I started crying for no apparent reason.

Nearing Christmas I was as blue as I could be. Why? No answer. We never celebrated Christmas.

So, was it because it was Hanukah? Christmas? Didn't know. On my way home from FATZ that evening I had another primal scream. This time it was in my car.

I was truly miserable during those holidays. Spanish music on the radio reminded me of San Diego. Everything reminded me of Victor.

Maybe the motive for my not eating, for not having an appetite was that I would rather lose weight and have a new body to go with my new life. Or maybe it was because Victor couldn't eat anymore.

Susan and I started to plan a trip to Ireland. We both felt that I needed to travel again. And I said I would go anywhere that I didn't go with Victor. That left only a few countries.

We decided to go to Ireland. David and his family had been there the past summer and David spoke about what a lovely visit they had in Dublin and Scotland.

Still, I didn't want to have a good time or even get excited about going because I felt I shouldn't have a good time without Victor. Once again, having a good time made me feel guilty.

Still, I told myself that I had made it through the past six months and I would probably get through my New Year's Day Party, as well. And if that was the case, I would make it through the trip to Ireland, also.

I went back to talking to Victor. This time I told him, I didn't know what his death was like but this life I was living was not worth living. Oh Victor if you only knew how much I miss you, I added.

For years, Victor and I had given a New Year's Day Party. My feeling about life had always been, find an excuse to celebrate. And, if none was available create a reason to celebrate. That's how we started the tradition of our New Year's Day party.

So it was that the first New Year's Day after Victor's Death, I invited and prepared for the party. It was with a heavy heart but I did it and really in the end, I was not sorry that I did.

Nevertheless, just shopping at SAMS upset me. I was nervous, emotional.

Finding where in the garage Victor had stored the leaves and covers for the table and putting then on the table troubled me.

Putting the table together, and remembering Victor doing this with me last year was emotional.

Everything was. With each glass or dish I put on the table, I remembered. This glass was bought on our trip to Barbados; this one was from London; these were from Spain; and that one was from his Jr. High School reunion.

My daughter, Lynne, and her family came from Jackson, and my daughter Susan came from Nashville We celebrated the fact that we were all together for this occasion.

My guests were pleased that I carried on the tradition. I was pleased that I was able to find the courage to do it.

CHAPTER 31

Unveiling

Why do we look for the sun at midnight?

Years earlier during an interview I had with Major Saad Haddad, the leader of the Southern Lebanese Christian Army, he posed that rhetorical question to me. While preparing for the unveiling of Victor's stone that phrase came to mind. Why indeed?

As the date for the unveiling got closer I found myself thinking of the days when Victor was dying. He had such a short time. A blessing for him, thank God; for that I was grateful. But for me the time was short and not enough of it.

I had decided that his tombstone should read, "Victor Zager, A Righteous Man." That was what David told his father as his father was dying. It was appropriate both then and for Victor's stone. Still, I was apprehensive.

The difficulty was going through the ordeal of picking the stone, making sure everything was done correctly and worrying about how I was going to emotionally handle the unveiling and simply going through the process.

True, Susan and David were doing most of the work but every time I thought about the unveiling, my stomach pain got worse and I became more teary-eyed.

My dream during that time: Victor was back, alive, and I was so glad to see him that I kissed his face over and over again. Susan was standing next to him, his hair in my mouth. Even in the dream, I wondered what that was all about.

I told him I was worried about what he would wear as I had given most of his clothes away. But the family never finished the job so there were still some of his clothes in the downstairs closet. However, there was no underwear. So I suggested he buy two pairs. He could wear one and I would wash the other. When I woke, I had to laugh at the dream.

However, unlike the dream, reality was that Susan and I fought over the etching on the gravestone. That was not funny. I wanted the letters z"l next to his name. Those letters stood for zichrono lebracha, a traditional Hebrew phrase meaning, "may his memory be a blessing." Susan thought it ruined the look. Still, she felt guilty for questioning anything I wanted. But she was designing it and had a talent for such things. Nevertheless, I became entrenched. Insisting it had to be done my way. Perhaps it was because I had to fight about something.

For me the argument became a real emotional setback. I couldn't sleep, I had terrible stomach pains and I felt guilty about putting all of that on Susan. Finally, I relented. Do what you want, I told her. I added the words that in the end it doesn't matter. And I realized that it was true. In the end nothing matters.

She redrew the sketch for the stone and felt that it now looked good. By then I was in such a deep funk it took lots of energy just to try to get out of the depression. I was miserable.

And I knew Victor would have been livid. Fighting over the gravestone would have made him very angry because it was so inappropriate.

Finally, the gravestone was approved by David, Susan, Lynne and me. And with that approval rather than relief, a foreboding engulfed me; the date was getting closer.

So, the closer it got to Passover and the unveiling, the more nervous, teary-eyed and emotional I got. Thinking about it was not good for my health. But I couldn't turn off the thoughts.

I really don't know how I got through the week and I positively don't know how I got through the weekend before I had to leave for that event.

At FATZ the day before I left, the support group there really cared for me. The love they poured out to me, helped. One of the managers told me that all the staff was there for me and added that it was all right to be upset. And the manager reiterated what Barbara had said: I had people praying and worrying about me. Even though the restaurant was very crowded and the staff was very busy they nevertheless came over to talk to me, to try to cheer me, tried to make me laugh. All of it helped.

The morning I left for the airport I cried even during my workout. I also felt what I often felt. I wished I was dead.

On the flight I couldn't stop crying. Thinking. Visualizing us in wonderful places. And feeling as if I was going back to bury him once again.

In the past, he stood by me – but he was not with me anymore.

Heaven knew how melancholy I was. How sad and morose.

At the Passover Seder, I could not participate. It was far too difficult to even breathe and to listen to the words. I could not speak.

Nevertheless, despite my trepidations the unveiling turned out to be a dignified and meaningful event. And I was able to conduct myself appropriately.

The weather was positively beautiful, sunny and warm. All the week before there were tornados, high winds and rain. But that day was perfect.

And when the unveiling was over, I felt as if that was the last thing I was able to do for him. There was nothing else I could do. Sad but true. What else was left for me to do for him? And in the end, I was grateful it all turned out so well.

It was a form of closure, I was told. But I didn't feel closed at all. Maybe it was time to let go but I guess I didn't want to let go or was not ready. Perhaps I would never be ready.

The one who shared the life's moments that came flooding back to me was gone. There was no one else. That life was over.

At one point during the service, I looked around and wondered: How did I get here? My son, a grandfather; me a great-grandmother. None of what I was now living seemed real.

On my way home I stopped at the Delta Lounge in Atlanta. Serving at the bar in the lounge was a woman I had seen there before. She always remembered that I drank white wine and always remembered to bring me a glass of ice.

The first time I stopped into that lounge after burying Victor, she had asked about him. Now she asked how I was doing. I told her I was doing fine.

I think when Victor died people expected me to shrivel up and die; to hide from people. I wanted to do that. But I couldn't do that. I had to live because Victor would have been very disappointed in me. I couldn't disappoint Victor.

So, after he died, after the unveiling, I dressed carefully, put on my makeup and pasted a smile on my face. All because I wanted Victor to be proud of me.

CHAPTER 32

Insights

As hard as starting a new life was, it nevertheless revealed some interesting insights.

For example: while remembering our great many travels together I was also reminded about how Victor and I approached those travels. We always said that we would go while we still could. And added: Who knows how much longer we can continue to do this? How true that was.

Beginning when Victor was in the hospital, I had been jotting down my feelings, thoughts and reactions dealing with Victor's death. I found that writing gave me an outlet for some of the emotional baggage I was carrying and it gave me the opportunity to vent.

In addition, along with people's reactions to me and what I was going through, I tried to look at all of this new life I was leading from a different perspective. That is, I was trying to be objective. Or at least trying to look at the experience while not being IN the experience. When I was writing it felt like watching someone else going through all of it.

One day I discovered that I was accountable to no one but myself. I was astounded. This was a new concept and a new state for me to be in.

The revelation made me wonder if that was a good thing. At the time, I thought it probably wasn't.

But the reason I was shocked was that Victor always gave me free reign. Never said, do this or do that. He might suggest, "I would do it this way. I might do such and thus. If I were you I wouldn't do that." But he never stopped me from being me. He never acted as if I was accountable to him for my actions. Maybe I thought I was and now realized that I wasn't. But when you are a couple you are each accountable to each other. When you are alone, you are accountable to no one but yourself.

And I realized that Victor was so very proud of me, of anything I accomplished. Even the small and unimportant things like when I won at solitaire while we were flying overseas. He proudly called the stewardess over to see my win.

Or if I gave a lecture, you could see the pride in his face. Or while signing books; when we owned the newspaper; when he talked to others about me. On those occasions he always referred to himself as "Muriel's Husband" as if that was his only identity.

So why did I now feel as if I was accountable to no one but myself? Because for me, it was a new experience. Also, the idea of not being accountable to any one other than myself suddenly frightened me. Too much responsibility, I thought.

Another thing I learned was that within the confines of my home, I was content. How can I describe that feeling? For one thing I really hated to leave the house. I had to force myself out of it. And I did so because I knew if I didn't I'd probably wind myself up in a ball of sadness and never go anywhere.

Still, there was something very comforting for me to curl up in my own house, in my own bed.

Memories kept flooding into my mind. And although it was nostalgic, miserable, and sad for me to relive those happy moments, it was also a feeling of satisfaction in the knowledge that we had shared those times. But it was devastating to realize that there was no one else in this world who could share those past times and memories.

I suppose that was why I experienced again and again so many happy occasions in the privacy of my home. Memories would also engulf me everywhere else. Quite often, a memory would jump into my mind for no apparent reason. Still, the memories were more comforting when they came to me at home. Maybe it was because we spent so much time there together. I really don't know. I have no answers. I only have questions.

I adamantly replied NO when someone asked me if I was moving nearer to my Nashville family or moving anywhere else. Leaving home would mean leaving Victor behind and REALLY walking alone. At least in the confines of my home, I had the memories, the objects, the consolation that my past life actually existed. True, it no longer did, but it had been real for many years. I didn't want to wipe it all away.

And I seemed obsessed with keeping the house clean and orderly and with keeping myself looking my best when I went out. And I positively fixated over making the perfect bed each morning. Pillow shams and all. I felt that was because we had such a good time in that bed.

Also, I made a point of smiling in public. Of laughing and making jokes. I reasoned that people would not mind being with me if I wasn't morose. Therefore, I was often told what fun it was to be with me. I began to feel as if I was playacting the part of the Merry Widow. Maybe I was.

Because I carried myself with dignity most people told me how strong I was and how well I was coping. The truth may have been otherwise, but it helped to get me through it all.

But it was the kindnesses that made me cry. Like a friend we had met in Spain during the 9/11 experience. He sent a card from Spain when he was visiting there again. He hadn't forgotten Victor and me. Acknowledging that I was now alone he wanted me to know that he was thinking of me and the time we all spent together.

An employee at Wal-Mart asked how I was doing. When I told her it was hard because of the special relationship Victor and I had, she said you could see that when you two were together. Those kind words made me cry.

I kept telling myself I was doing okay considering my condition; I thought of the state I was in, as a condition.

Everything took such an effort. Took all my energy. I had determined to accept any invitation offered. For years I had been counseling widows about doing exactly that. So I took my own advice. But following that advice was another matter.

Going out to a birthday dinner party for a friend was unbelievably difficult. Being alone in that crowd was the hardest part. It was a very lovely party with a terrific hostess and host, the house was simply magnificent, the couple had three gorgeous children, and there were a number of close friends there.

I had on my pasted smile, made lots of witty remarks and left as soon as it seemed appropriate. That night I discovered that I am a better actress than I originally thought. I had one face for the world and one for when I was alone. It felt like the two masks associated with acting - Drama/Comedy.

When I finally set a new daily routine, one of the first things I did was arrange my activities differently. I now awoke early, when I slept at all, made coffee, took a cup back to bed and read for hours.

I followed that by going for my workouts later than I used to in the morning. That way I could avoid seeing people I knew. One morning at the YMCA a woman whom I didn't know stopped me to say she had to tell me what a great guy Victor was and how she thinks about me all the time and wondered about how I was doing.

"He was such a great guy," she said. She also asked if I saw the plaque at the FATZ restaurant.

Victor touched so many people's lives. Like that woman I didn't know at the YMCA. And I had at least one encounter like that each day. In the end, there was no way to avoid people, no matter how I tried.

My encounters only served to prove what I had always said: there's good and bad in everything. The good was the fact that Victor touched so many lives; the bad was that he was gone.

CHAPTER 33

Home Alone One Year Later

Someone asked, "Aren't you afraid or concerned about living alone in that big house?"

My answer was: Why should I be? What's the worst thing that can happen to me? Someone will kill me? So what? I'll die. Since Victor died, death is not a problem for me.

But then I asked myself, "Do you really want to die?" My answer surprised me. I answered no. So I told myself, if that is true then shut up and live.

Besides I loved my house because Victor was in every corner of it.

During our life together Victor taught me that nothing remains the same. Everything changes. And so it was with Victor's death.

Victor. Even in death Victor meant life.

Time now had a whole new meaning. What time was it? What day was it? Somehow it didn't matter. Nothing mattered.

When sleep came, it came. When it didn't. It didn't.

When I was here (wherever that might be) I wanted to be there. When I was there I wanted to be here. When I was nowhere I wanted to be somewhere. When I was somewhere I wanted to be nowhere.

I was on a ride. Barbara explained that my emotions were like being on an amusement park ride that flings you from one place to another.

At 7:00 a.m. one morning I realized it was one year since he died. He died at 7:00 a.m. and I spent that day reliving the days before his death; those days in the hospital. It was the first time I had done that.

The day of his death, one year later was, in some ways, harder than the actual day he died. Reminiscing was very emotional. Reliving his death was extremely painful.

Focusing on 7:00 a.m. I once again watched him dying. And remembered that on that day he waited until Susan and I turned away for just a second. That's when he left us.

He was always considerate. So, being considerate, he died in that second when we weren't watching.

I was so grateful that at least I was with him when he died.

On that first anniversary, people called to say they remembered him. From near and far, they called. Flowers came from the family: red and pink roses. Irma and Norman, close friends, sent white lilies.

I had lunch with Barbara, and dinner with Dave Morin who had become a close friend.

Somehow I got through that day. Once again, I survived. May my life prove that love is stronger than death, I prayed.

My exterminator told me he thought God leaves the one who can take it the best. He said Victor was a strong man but he could not have survived without me. Somehow, his words gave me comfort.

Make everyone laugh. That was my motto. Even though I was miserable.

That day I received an email from a contact Victor had in the Pentagon. He had just learned about Victor's death.

In the email he said, "I am so sorry for your loss. I did not know that Victor died. He would come to the Pentagon and visit with me from time to time, or he would sometimes call me on the telephone.

"Victor shared stories of some of the times he and you shared. Clearly, he was a man in love. I always enjoyed his visits and telephone calls. I wish you the best. Please accept my sincere condolences."

Things like that email made me weep. But the knowledge that we shared a love that was so special gave me strength.

When people told me I would make it through this life. I determined they were crazy. I could only hope to get through each day.

And the days were very long; I thought they'd never end. But somehow the year went by quickly. Maybe I would survive after all.

CHAPTER 34

State Of Limbo

Question: What part of my life did I not share with him?
Answer: No part. Nothing. Nada

During this state of limbo I had been in from the time Victor died, felt as if I was in hell. Bitter, hard, heavy tears and oh, the pain.

Some days I felt I was going to make it. I just wasn't sure I wanted to.

Crying myself to sleep almost every night assured me I was still in a state of limbo.

One night when I left FATZ as I was looking up at the plaque with his picture and silently saying a goodnight to Victor, the song, "You were meant for me" started whirling around in my head.
You were meant for me. I was meant for you. I could barely see to drive the car home.

I had taken to greeting his plaque when I entered FATZ and saying goodbye to him when I left. Somehow that seemed fitting.

Funny, I thought, that he should be immortalized with a plaque in a restaurant, a tribute at a corporation website, and on a paperweight, in a photo of him in his tuxedo sitting next to a friend's teenage son at a Heart Association event.

Someone who was very close to Victor took me to lunch to talk about Victor. It was a kindness and I appreciated it, but it was another person to console.

Cards, emails and calls kept coming from Florida; London; Israel, all over the planet.

Barbara explained that my mourning was very much like what I had described going through during the Jewish Holy Days, The Days of Awe.
And one day, she pronounced me sane. Being with her weekly was truly like having a therapy session. She was so good for me. She helped me through the difficult journey I was on.

Of all those I was consoling, family, friends, strangers, I was the one who lost the most. I found that ironic.

One person said I looked good. Another one said I was doing good. So if everything was so good, I wondered, how come everything was so miserable?

I wished I could figure out what it was it that made me know during our first encounter that Victor was my soul mate. And on the other hand, I never figured out what he saw in me.

Funny thing happened to me on another day. I was remembering when Victor was dying, when I asked him to take me with him. I meant it then, but I suddenly realized that despite my pain and despite my suffering, somehow, I really wanted to live. It was different this time. Because I knew that despite my unhappiness, I did not want to die.

Bill, a friend who worked at the airline counter in my area sent me an email saying that he felt, "Victor got his nickel's worth out of life." That reminded me of when Victor was dying I told him that our life together was quite a ride. He said, "Yeah, two kids from Brooklyn."

With not eating I found I was losing weight. I never thought I would live long enough to worry about losing weight, having spent a lifetime concerned about gaining weight. Now I needed to concentrate on eating.

Interesting phenomenon: If I tried to force a memory or a place it was difficult to conjure up in my mind. But memories came seemingly by themselves and seemingly at random.

So many things reminded me of something else; but everything reminded me of Victor and our shared life. In my mind's eye, I saw so many scenes that we had lived through together. It was a wonderful life and I was grateful for it.

CHAPTER 35

A Year And A Half Later

I was still going to sleep every night saying to myself, I can't believe I survived another day.

But life and I went on.

I even seemed to be sleeping better. Seeing the bed at night made me aware that at least I made it through another day.
And I still had vivid images flashed on the widescreen in my head.
Continued to see us together on the trips we took.

My appetite for food and sex was still missing.
Our joy with food and lovemaking had been active and good up until the week before he died.
The fact that there were things I knew about him, things he knew about me that nobody else knew or could ever know, still troubled me.

I would have given anything just to be back in his arms once again.

I often told him that I wanted to dedicate one of my books to him. I wanted my dedication in my last novel to read: To Victor, who makes everything possible. He wouldn't hear of it.

We had not only loved one another, we genuinely liked each other.

Many times at home alone I again cried uncontrollably. Wiped the tears, put a face on, smiled and went out to face the world.

Thoughts that invaded my mind centered on: Why am I here?

But I kept a busy social calendar. And it was true: God sends you people when you need them.
And every once in a while I believed I was making it.

I went to the Imaging Center for a mammogram one morning a year and a half later and I completely lost it.
The women's health center where I used to get my mammogram moved to the Imaging Center where Victor had his CT scan and where it was determined he had cancer. He died ten days later.

I walked into the place and completely lost control. Couldn't stop crying. The tears just poured out. Didn't stop until two hours later. Luckily the technician remembered the incident and understood my reaction.

Some mornings I would awake thinking I'm never going to get through this day. And sometimes later in the day, I marveled at the fact that I did.

As a child I was in a skit where the punch line was, "You call this a life?"

Now, as a widow, I heard that line quite often in my head. I was existing from day to day. But 'you call this a life' I asked myself?

After all, Victor was my lover, my confidant, my best friend and my conscience.

About one month before Victor's birthdate approached, the second one after his death, I found that I was jumpy and nervous. My mother always said we worry about the wrong things.

Victor's birthday wasn't the most painful. It was what I learned just a few days before Victor's birthday.

Our son, David, had esophageal cancer.

As horrible as that revelation was, the anguish was made even worse because I had to go through that nightmare alone. Victor could not share in my agony. We could not go through this together.

I was alone.

CHAPTER 36

Now What?

He was my anchor and now I found myself adrift. Where do I go from here?

If I could watch Victor die and watch David going through his disease, I felt I could put on my makeup, put on my smile and go out into the world.

I kept my column going on schedule because Victor was so very proud of that column. Even as he lay dying I told him I got my column out and a big smile crossed his face. He was very pleased.

Sometimes I felt as if I was moving on. Other times I felt as if I was spinning my wheels. That was an expression Victor often used. Somehow it fit.

Friends started sending me reading material dealing with death. They thought it might help. I cried through most of those books. Someone even gave me two books dealing with the hereafter: "Do Dead People Walk Their Dogs?" And "Do Dead People Watch You In The Shower." Those theories were impossible for me to accept.

And I still had a few peculiar episodes: One drop of water fell from the bedroom ceiling and it made me wonder; one drop from the kitchen ceiling, and again I wondered; a light flicking on the bathroom lighting made me wonder; suddenly smelling his scent; was there a way the dead could communicate with the living?

One day my housekeeper claimed she felt Victor's presence in the bedroom. It made her cry. There were times when I wanted to believe Victor was trying to communicate with me. But those times were few and far between. I was too rational.

Who knows? I thought. Don't dismiss any idea.

I was hanging some freshly laundered clothes in my closet one day when I suddenly saw, like a flash in my memory, an image of Victor buying biscotti's at the bakery we frequented in Florence. I wondered why that came to me at that moment. There was nothing in that closet to remind me of Florence, or a bakery or anything remotely connected to that memory.

Keep a busy social calendar, I told myself. And I did.

God sends you people when you need them, I told myself again and again. New people came into my life and helped me through the rough times. And I reminded myself that the people I expected would be there were not necessarily there for me.

And there was no escape from the pain. And, with David so gravely ill, the thought of what may yet come, at times overwhelmed me.

Half of what went on in the world I didn't see; half of what went on in the world I didn't hear. I was so out of focus. Maybe it's better that way, I thought.

I didn't mind drinking alone, it was sleeping alone that I objected to.

Funny, after a couple of glasses of wine I felt as if I had enough to eat – even if I had eaten nothing. Drinking alcohol was supposed to be a stimulant to eating. Reverse was the effect on me.

Some nights I just wanted to cry for my loss; for what I had lost. Yes, I knew I should have been grateful for what I had, and I was, but I wanted more.

Suddenly driving around the curve of my driveway one evening I was remembering the day I first saw my house. Through heavy tears, I remembered Victor driving me to view the house. That had been more than thirty years before.

I thought I was okay for a little while one day but I was not. It seemed to be getting worse, not better. A good friend said it would never get better. I knew she was right.

All the books I had read said that there were several stages of mourning. For me, there were not even different stages. I didn't go through the denial, the anger, or the bargaining. For me the only two steps that applied were acceptance and depression.

Do you believe in heaven and hell I was often asked? No. You make your own heaven and hell right here on earth. Except I sometimes thought Victor might be in heaven, but I was in hell.

Looking at my wedding band brought back another memory. Bought it at Spitzer and Furman, a jewelry store we stopped at when on a cruise to the Caribbean.

When we returned to the ship we entered a costume/talent show.

Victor was dressed as the master of ceremonies. I wore a black bathing suit with jewelry pinned all over the suit. And I had a sign that said, "Spritzer and Furman, where are you?"

Went to Rhythm and Roots, a festive gathering of bands down a closed Main Street in my hometown. All I could think of was the similarities to the same type of thing (sans the Blues Bands) going on in Frankfurt, Baracas, Barcelona, Amsterdam, Florence, etc.

We were on route to Atlanta On a flight from Madrid September 11th when the Twin Towers were hit and our plane was ordered to the nearest airport.

We landed in the Azores. We were a jumbo jet and loaded with passengers. The Azores could not have handled so many people on a normal flight. And we were not normal. But the people on the island could not have been nicer. Opening their homes because there were not enough beds in accommodations.

We had no clothes, medicines, etc. The baggage compartment couldn't be opened. The druggist opened his pharmacy to supply medication to those who needed it.

We spent two days there before returning to Madrid. It was quite an experience.

Thanks to the Captain who told us we were now a family, and we became a family in those few hours. Alberto, a young man we met on the flight who was born in Spain and the Captain kept in touch all those years.

Alberto was so sweet and kind when he called and said such lovely things about Victor and me. Then he told me all about his latest trip to Spain to see his mother, and his family. That year he again returned to the States on September 11th.

I received a condolence letter from a couple we had not seen in forty years. They had heard the news from a mutual friend.

They, too, praised Victor and reminded me of the happy times we spent together.

I learned that it was true. Laughter goes a long way when one is out with others. I saved my depression for when I was alone.

At this late age I had to learn to live alone. I had never lived by myself before.

I was getting calls from all over the world for a long time following his death expressing condolences.

Could you have gone on without me better than I am doing without you, I kept asking him? I doubt it, I answered for him. But who knows?

The longer I went without him, the more I relished being alone in my bedroom with my vivid memories and dreams of Victor. The two places I felt closest to Victor were in a plane and in our bed.

Some days I felt as if I was on an Island, alone. I became an obsessive reader. It was my great escape. I realized that I was creating a new life.

Now, in this new journey I was on, for good or bad, I discovered that there is life after death.

Not his. Mine.

"Each person is really only half complete and it is only when partnered with another is he whole." Parshat Pekudei

Epilogue

When Victor died I thought I had lost everything.

Then I learned I had more to lose.

The news came a few days after my son David's birthday as I was preparing my column. David called and told me that he was diagnosed with the same thing Uncle Stanley, Victor's brother, died of. Esophageal cancer.

David went in for tests on his 57th birthday and learned the news.

He decided to go to Anderson in Houston, Texas and he would be staying with friends. David was to see the head of the department the next day.

David also told me that Susan, my youngest daughter, was already on her way from Nashville to my home in Bristol.

She would call me from the airport. They didn't want me to be alone.

He told me not to tell my other daughter, Lynne, as he wanted to be the one to break the news to each member of the family.

Beverly, the eldest granddaughter was on her way to New York so that she could be with her sister, Lexi, when David broke the news to his youngest daughter.

David explained that Jenny and Ron were on their way to Knoxville so that they could be with David Aaron, when David broke the news to his son David Aaron.

Mark, another son who was at school at Vanderbilt in Nashville, was being picked up and brought home so that he could be told.

David asked me to be strong. I promised I would be.

I called Sally, a good friend. She came immediately and stayed with me until Susan arrived at the airport. Then Sally went to pick her up. It was just as well. I couldn't have driven to the airport. I could not stop shaking.

Susan stayed with me until she left for L.A. and her oncologist appointment a few days later. I left for a preplanned trip to friends in Florida. It was Victor's birthday and I didn't want to be alone. Now more than ever, I didn't want to be alone.

When I returned home from Florida I waited for the news from David who was still in Texas at Anderson. I couldn't seem to bring myself to go out. I wanted to curl up in bed with a bottle.

The next few days were a blur.
Murray and Rita took me out to dinner.
I canceled dinner with other friend

Couldn't do exercise. Had trouble eating. Sleeping.
This was every parent's worst nightmare.

Jocelyn (Stanley's widow) was told and called me immediately. Just like when we buried Victor, she was there. Once again I thought it interesting how God sends people when you need them. She told me one must have hope.

Heard from cousins I rarely speak with.

Went into a deep depression. Couldn't leave the house. Drank lots of wine. Couldn't even get drunk.

Didn't want to see anyone.

Finally forced myself out of the deep funk and forced myself to see friends for lunch. I decided I had to keep healthy, so as not to burden the family any more than they already were.

Two weeks later, I was still trying to go to the YMCA to do some exercise. I told myself I must force myself to go. But I decided I would postpone going so that I didn't have to see people, put on a happy face. It was just too difficult.

It felt as if I was reliving the nightmare with Victor. David had a CT scan two months earlier. Nothing showed.

Now it had spread, it was aggressive. Just like Victor.

Susan commented that it's not fair. Who ever said life was fair? I countered. I knew from experience that life is not fair. I even used that phrase in my first novel.

The time and David's cancer were both moving very fast. It felt as if I was losing him by the day. I was terrified.

We didn't know the reason for David's weight loss was the cancer. He was dieting. Thought he was doing a great job. We worry about the wrong things, like my mother used to say.

This was the first time in my life I wanted to commit suicide.

I asked myself: is it true that I don't want to live or have I been using the excuse for living because I have to go on for the family. Is that the truth? Or even in these miserable times was it that I didn't want to die?

If he dies, I remunerated, I don't know if I have enough HAZAK (the Hebrew word for strength that Victor left me with) to go on.

More days of hell,
Victor help, I screamed to the empty house many times.

I realized I was right to push myself out when Victor died. But this time I didn't leave the house for days. I simply could not.

Thanksgiving was hard. Extremely hard. There were thirty of us at the Nashville table. Everyone wanted to see and be with David.

During that time I had some special alone moments with David. He discussed arranging for funds for the children's education, his will, my will, his practice and what to do about it. He talked about the future of his family. He was putting his house in order.

He spoke of these things as contingencies in case the treatment didn't work. David told me that if it didn't work they would probably try "more radical" treatment, like experimental drugs.

David also talked about how unfair this was. Once again I used the line: Who says life is fair? What else could I say?

In my mind I relived his birth; the pet names we had for him when he was a baby; we used to call him Duvey Duveshoes, and Davey Zager, King of the Wild Frontier.

If ever I missed Victor surely it was now. Dealing with David's illness had been unbearably difficult; made more so because I was alone.

After the second treatment one of his tumors appeared to be shrinking. There seemed to be hope.

I told him to look upon his treatments as a path, a road to recovery. But there had to be a light at the end of that tunnel. And there wasn't.

And, as this was Chanukah, the Festival of Lights, the celebration of a miracle, I had to believe that there was a miracle out there for David.

Susan's strength and research not only kept David going it helped all of us to cope.

What do you feel? What do you say? When your son says he's training his 20 year-old son to help you with your finances if he's not around?

You say nothing. It just breaks your heart.

After four months of treatment, the treatment didn't work. He had a blockage treated with Botox on his larynx. His voice sounded better.

They were going to start treating him with experimental drugs in a couple of weeks.

I was watching him slowly dying. But I had to have hope. Without hope, I would be lost.

Still, I now was just floating through the days and nights. I had no structure in my life. I, who always had a schedule, was completely out of a routine. My only focal point was David.

When I was at his home for Passover – an extremely tough emotional trip- we spoke about the soul. He explained that the reference to the soul living after death was in the Bible. Because the soul is a part of God, it cannot die, he told me.

But physically when he walked a flight of stairs he couldn't catch his breath. Had to sit down to rest.

One day, he walked inside the house from the patio and fell to his knees. I went over to him; he looked at me as if he didn't know who I was.

Nevertheless, he dressed in a suit and tie, and we went to his office to sign my new Will. He looked great, was in complete command and handled himself as if he weren't ill.

I signed my new Will making his portion of my estate to go to the Estate of David Zager. It took all my strength not to burst into tears.

When he got home he was exhausted and had to rest on the couch.

When I returned to my own home in Bristol after Passover, I was listless, depressed and just wasted my days.

I was told that if he took the experimental drug the good thing was that he wouldn't be getting a placebo.

The bad thing was that it hadn't been tried on humans.

It didn't matter. None of those things mattered in the end. He didn't qualify.

Now he and his wife had to decide whether to go into a different chemotherapy or do nothing that would affect his quality of life.

My daughter-in-law told my daughter, Susan, to enjoy the time we have. We have the rest of our lives to cry.

In April, David his wife, Lynne and Toby, Susan and I went to New York to celebrate a dear friend's birthday. Allan was the friend who was at Victor's hospital bed when Victor was dying. It was a wonderful time for the family, even though David was in a wheelchair and had to rest a good deal of the time.

While flying home from that marvelous family weekend I thought: Wouldn't it be great if my plane crashed and I died? I wouldn't have to deal with what I had to face and the family could be content because we had such a warm family weekend.

But while I wanted to die, David was so full of life. His sharp sense of humor never left him.

Watching him die; watching him in a wheelchair. Horrible.

Mothers Day I went to Nashville to be with the family – really to be with David. He looked worse than he had two weeks earlier.

The decision to try another round of chemo was made and he started treatment. There seemed little hope. He was on oxygen; he couldn't eat; couldn't swallow; coughing up phlegm; he was sleepy and tired all the time; he'd lost his voice and I could barely hear him.

But he still hadn't lost his sense of humor. Joked about having received a six-pack that morning. He was referring to his oxygen. He said the good thing that came of the chemo was that his fungus infection that he'd had for twenty-five years had cleared up.

One day he craved a roast beef sandwich. Kitzi went to a restaurant called Noshville and got it for him. She placed half a sandwich in front of him.

He took a bite, gagged, threw up. Said he was sorry.

As a mother I'm supposed to kiss it and make it all better, I thought. Instead, I was watching my child dying, while I am living. It's not supposed to be that way.

He had a marvelous past and a wonderful future. All gone.

When I went to say goodbye he said, "Thank you mother for coming to spend Mother's Day with me." It broke my heart.

It was the last time I saw him.

David decided to not continue with any more treatment. The new round wasn't working He decided to go with the "quality of life" option.

He was trying so hard to live. He was clinging to life at any and every moment. He was trying to do everything for everybody. Everything in his power to forestall the inevitable. He was making jokes and laughing. He was trying to eat; trying to keep down his meds; rest. Anything. He still was making jokes.

But we all knew, as he did, that in the end he couldn't win this battle.

And all you have left when it's all over are the memories and the pictures.

Well the unthinkable happened. And on Father's Day.

What do you do on the day you learn your son is dead?

You cry. You cry A LOT.

You think of the day he was born.

You call friends who offer words admitting that words don't help. You look at the ironies.

You note that Victor died in June; David died in June. Two years almost to the day.

Victor and I had been married for 57 years when Victor died.
David was 57 years of age when he died.

You remember the happy times together with your son, especially the past year.

You remember the last words he said to you when you were together. You remember the last telephone conversation two days before.

You remember his smile.
You remember his sense of humor.
You remember how special he was; his knowledge of history, religion; economics, politics, religion. He was a fountain of knowledge.
And he built a warm loving family.
And he built a practice out of nothing.
And it's all gone...with him.

And you remember a whole lot more.
And then you cry again.

The will to go on doesn't get stronger the longer you live with these deaths. It actually lessens. Problem is there's no choice.

It's true that on a daily basis the one I miss most is my husband Victor. The one I can't bear the loss of is my son David.

I recently came across these words in the Holy Day Prayer Book that I felt really sums it all up:

Birth is the beginning,

Death is the destination,

Life is the journey.

Acknowledgements

My everlasting love and gratitude to:

Barbara Flynt-Wampler for helping me on my journey;

Bonnie Ardito who read every line at least twice;

Rita and Murray Scher, Janet and Larry Jayne, David Morin and Sally Bassett who became my life-lines;

And to the staff at FATZ;

Each of you helped me to survive.

Made in the USA
Lexington, KY
20 July 2018